KOREA
BETWEEN THE
WARS

A SOLDIER'S STORY

Fred Ottoboni

VINCENTE BOOKS INC
Sparks, Nevada

Library of Congress Card Catalog Number 96-34188
ISBN 0-915241-02-1

Production at Reno Printing, Inc.

Published by Vincente Books Inc.
P.O. Box 50704
Sparks, Nevada 89435-0704

Library of Congress Cataloging-in-Publication Data
Ottoboni, Fred, 1927—
    Korea between the wars : a soldier's story / Fred Ottoboni.
    p.   cm.
    Includes index.
    ISBN 0-915241-02-1 (pbk.)
    1. Ottoboni, Fred, 1927—   .   2. Korean War, 1950-1953--
Personal narratives, American.   I. Title.
DS921.6.O88   1996   96-34188
951.904'2--dc20   CIP

Printed in the United States of America

TABLE OF CONTENTS

PREFACE

While going through my mother's effects after her death in 1989, I found a shoe box filled with more than 200 letters I had written to my family decades before, during my tour of duty with the United States Army in Korea in 1947 and early 1948.

As I read the letters that I had written almost 50 years earlier, I felt their contents might be of interest to others. These letters tell not only of my personal experiences and views, but also describe the army unit of which I was a part. The condition of our military forces on the ground in South Korea during the occupation, although an important part of the history of the Korean War, has never, to my knowledge, been committed to writing. Yet it should be. While I was in Korea, American occupation forces were so handicapped that even I, an enlisted man only 19 years old, clearly noted that our forces, few in numbers, unwashed, poorly equipped, and untrained would be unable to resist, let alone cope with, an invasion by hostile forces from the north.

Discovery of the shoe box of letters planted the seeds for *Korea Between the Wars.* The plan of the book evolved slowly. A presentation of the letters in their entirety and in chronological arrangement would not only be confusing, but also incomplete. The letters describe, in an unorganized fashion, living conditions, friends, activities, work experiences, and feelings as they occurred to me at the moment of writing. The letters seldom give an indication of location in time or relationship to each other. They also do not tell the whole story. I recall that I usually tried to paint a picture of things rosier than they really were because I did not want to upset my mother. However, when I read my letters after the passage of so many years, I could not help but wonder what my perception of what would and would not upset her was at that time.

For ease of reading, I decided to tell the story of my time in Korea using unedited excerpts from my letters linked together with recollections refreshed by the letters. The last chapter recounts parts of the history of the post-World War II era in Asia that have helped me understand some of the events and experiences that were so inexplicable to me at the time.

A few of the many pictures made with my Kodak Brownie camera are included in the body of the text. Appendices are added to give a list of the books I found of immense value in helping me understand the history and events of the time, and a brief history of my army unit, the 63rd Infantry Regiment. The names of the many friends and acquaintances mentioned in my letters are included in an index.

The shoe box of letters I wrote so many years ago is a heartwarming memento of my mother's devotion to her children. She was a good and loving woman. I will be eternally grateful that she was my mother and that I was able to tell her while she was still with us how much I appreciated all she did for my brother and me.

Fred Ottoboni
January 1997

KOREA BETWEEN THE WARS

INTRODUCTION

This book is the story of an enlisted man who served in the United States Army of Occupation in South Korea during 1947 and part of 1948. It is a personal memoir that adds to the written history of South Korea in that it covers a time of great suffering and disappointment for the Korean people and presents a view of conditions in the United States Army in Korea during the critical period leading up to the start of the Korean War.

During the five years between the end of World War II in August of 1945 and the start of the Korean War in June of 1950, the relationship between the Soviet Union and the United States underwent dramatic change, from wartime allies to peacetime enemies. A cold war that lasted almost 50 years began. The Iron Curtain closed across Europe. The Berlin Airlift by the United States saved West Berlin from isolation and eventual occupation by the Soviet Army. And, the American-supported Chinese Nationalist Government and its army were defeated and driven from Mainland China by the Communist Chinese.

Today, we know that Korea presented an unanticipated problem for the United States when World War II ended. Korea had been an independent country for many hundreds of years until it was invaded and occupied in 1910 by Japanese forces, who treated the Korean people with great cruelty. The Japanese used Korea as a source of food and forced labor and as a staging area for invasions of Manchuria and China.

Korea was never a battlefield during World War II. Even so, when the Japanese were defeated, the Korean people were joyous and looked forward to liberation, independence, and the return of happier times. But these things did not happen. Korea was not liberated at the end of World War II, as the Korean people had hoped. Instead, tensions between the United States and the Soviet Union led to partition of the country.

Under a hastily-reached agreement between the United States and the Soviet Union, the northern half of Korea was occupied by troops from the Soviet Union and the southern half by troops from the United States. The conditions that led to this agreement and the problems that this agreement caused provide the background for the story in this book.

During World War II, the Soviet Union did not participate in the war against Japan but remained neutral, ostensibly because of the great demands of their own war against Germany. However, in 1945, as the war in Europe was ending, the Allies (including the Soviet Union) met at two major conferences; Yalta in February, and Potsdam in July. Agreements were reached at these conferences in which Korea was to be given full independence after an unspecified period of occupation by Soviet and American forces. During the period of occupation, Korean leadership was to be regenerated and the economy rehabilitated, Also not specified were the exact zones within Korea to be occupied by the forces of the Soviets and the Americans (Matloff, pages 526, 535).

At these conferences, the parties agreed that the Soviet Union would enter the war against Japan about three months after the end of the war with Germany. The reason for the delay was to provide reasonable time for the Soviets to move forces and supplies the very long distance from Europe to their eastern frontier. At the time of the conferences, the Americans did not anticipate an easy victory over Japan. To defeat Japan, the Americans expected they would have to invade the Japanese home islands and, at the same time, contain strong Japanese forces stationed in Manchuria and Korea. Thus, the Americans welcomed Soviet entry to the war with the hope that Soviet forces would engage and defeat the Japanese forces in Manchuria and Korea. This would shorten the war and reduce the heavy casualties expected among American forces that would be invading the Japanese home islands (Lee Suk Bok, page 1).

What the American planners did not consider, and perhaps did not know at that time, was that construction of the nuclear bomb was well underway and that its use would make a costly invasion of the Japanese home islands unnecessary. As we now know, the atomic bombs dropped on Hiroshima and Nagasaki by American B-29's on August 6 and 9, 1945, ended the war. At the same time, on August 9, the Soviet Union entered the war and attacked the Japanese in Manchuria. On the next day, Japan asked for peace. The formal surrender of Japan was signed on September 2, 1945.

The Japanese Army in Manchuria, faced with the pressure of a Soviet offensive and the fact that the Japanese govern-- ment was surrendering, lost interest in fighting and quickly collapsed. This opened the door for Soviet occupation of the entire Korean peninsula. In light of the fact that the conferences at Yalta and Potsdam had failed to define the specific zones of occupation in Korea for Soviet and American forces, the United States was faced with the decision of either taking quick action to stop the occupation of the entire Korean Peninsula by Soviet forces or accepting the loss of a foothold on the Asian mainland that was of strategic importance to the defense of Japan against further Soviet expansion.

At an urgent midnight meeting of the American high command in Washington, D.C. on August 10-11, 1945, staff members were given 30 minutes to develop an order that would define the occupation zones in Korea. With no time to waste, the 38th parallel was selected as the dividing line. It was decided that Soviet forces would occupy the zone north of this east-west line and the American forces would occupy the zone south of it.

Given the circumstances of that midnight meeting, the selection of the 38th parallel was the only possible answer. The parallel was easy to see and lay out on a map; it included the capitol, Seoul, in the American zone; and it divided the country into northern and southern zones that were approximately the same size.

The disadvantage of this line, not foreseen at that time, was that it formed an unnatural boundary. It indiscriminately cut through provinces, villages, farms, and long-used routes of commerce, and separated the industrial north with its coal and electrical power from the agricultural southern part of the country. The Soviets agreed with this arrangement and Soviet forces proceeded to occupy and accept the surrender of Japanese forces in the northern zone. American forces were quickly sent from Okinawa to carry out the same tasks in the southern zone of Korea (Lee Suk Bok, page 4).

General John Hodge, a brave and dedicated officer, was selected as Commanding General, U.S. Army Forces in Korea, and assigned the 24th Corps, which included the 6th, 7th, and 40th Infantry Divisions, as the occupation force. In this assignment, General Hodge reported directly to General Douglas MacArthur in Japan who was then the Supreme Commander of American Forces in the Far East. History indicates that the War Department (today known as the Department of Defense) had no long-term plans or objectives for the occupation forces that were being sent to Korea. The immediate missions assigned to General Hodge were to disarm and repatriate Japanese nationals and preserve law and order until the Koreans were able to take over the government.

The first American troops, part of the 7th Infantry Division, arrived at the port city of Inch'on on September 8, 1945. These troops took over Seoul, and occupied key areas immediately south of the 38th parallel to ensure that Soviet troops did not enter the American zone. The 40th Infantry Division arrived at the southern port city of Pusan later in September, and occupied the extreme southeastern part of the Korean Peninsula. The 40th Infantry was decommissioned several months later, and played no further role in the occupation of Korea. In early October, the 6th Infantry Division arrived at Inch'on from the Philippine Islands, and occupied strategic points in the southern half of South Korea.

Serious errors were made from the beginning of the American occupation, and these continued until the start of the Korean War in June, 1950. The first was a directive from General MacArthur to General Hodge to keep the Japanese Governor-General in power, along with his Japanese administrators and Japanese police. This order from MacArthur conflicted with the initial directive from the American Military Joint Chiefs of Staff which, in effect, said no Japanese should be allowed to hold any position of responsibility or influence in Korea (Smith, page 15).

Another regrettable mistake occurred as the first American troops were disembarking at Inch'on. A large crowd of happy Koreans had gathered nearby to welcome and cheer the American troops as they marched by. The Japanese police, who were still in power by order of General MacArthur, fired their rifles into the crowd to maintain order. American military officers, perhaps obeying orders, supported this Japanese behavior (Smith, page 16).

The friendly American policy toward the hated Japanese outraged the Korean people so severely that, after a period of weeks, President Truman was forced to order General MacArthur to replace the Japanese with Koreans or Americans as quickly as possible. As a result, the Japanese Governor-General in Korea was replaced by General Archibald Arnold, Commander of the 7th Infantry Division in Korea. At the same time, General Arnold was also made the Military Governor of South Korea under General Hodge, and a two-month long process of removing the Japanese from positions of power in Korea began (Lee Suk Bok, page 7).

Problems persisted through 1946. The Japanese police were removed, but replaced by Japanese-trained Koreans who continued the brutal ways of the Japanese. The Korean rice crop was bought up by speculators and sold outside the country. As a result, many Koreans starved during the winter of 1945-46.

In early 1946, in an attempt to deal with civilian unrest, a Korean military force of about 50,000 men, the Korean Constabulary, was created by the U.S. Military Government. The American practice of giving preference to former Japanese officers in forming the constabulary alienated it from the civilian population. As a result, the constabulary was feared and not respected by the Korean people.

In October 1946, in Taegu, the South Korean railroad workers union, in protest against low wages and lack of food, refused to work. Because of their own starvation diet and police brutality against railroad workers, the people of Taegu joined the protest. The resulting riot spread throughout South Korea, and was responsible for the deaths of 60 police and an uncounted number of civilians.

In an attempt to prevent further starvation, a rice collection and rationing program for the 1946-47 harvest season was set up by the U.S. Military Government in Korea.

Under this program, the U.S. Military Government attempted to collect forcibly the rice production and to redistribute it among the population of South Korea. This program was not successful, probably due to lack of adequate manpower and equipment. Thus, once again, during the winter of 1946-47, Koreans were beset by a severe shortage of their major food source, rice.

The rice shortages added to the political turmoil in which many political parties, including a very large Communist Party and even some small private armies, sought power. Before 1946 ended, the U.S. Military Government in Korea was forced to use American occupation forces to quell undesirable political activity, and General MacArthur decreed the death penalty for anyone who resisted the Military Government.

During this time, the 7th Infantry Division was attempting to guard the approximately 150-mile mountainous frontier between North and South Korea. One of its jobs was to prevent subversives and raiding parties from crossing the border. As Korean Constabulary units became available, they were increasingly used to help guard this frontier. Even so, the border was seldom quiet. Korean communists infiltrated from North Korea to join communist groups in South Korea. There were frequent raids, fire fights, and unauthorized border crossings by Koreans from both sides of the 38th parallel. The infiltrations, raids, and fire fights along the 38th parallel continued until the Korean War started in June of 1950.

Further south, during 1946, the 6th Infantry Division completed its job of disarming and repatriating all Japanese nationals. Division personnel also finished collecting and destroying Japanese arms and ammunition, and the three regiments of the 6th Division coalesced and moved to key cities. At the end of 1946, the 1st Infantry Regiment was located at Taegu in the southeast, the 20th Infantry Regiment in Kwangju in the southwest, and the 63rd Infantry Regiment near Kunsan, a small seaport on the Yellow Sea, in the west-central part of South Korea.

The 63rd Infantry Regiment occupied a relatively quiet area about 150 miles south of the 38th parallel. Some undesirable political activity and violence occurred, but it never involved American troops. This was true despite the fact that soldiers, often alone or in small groups, guarded military property in rural and urban areas far from their base camps. All the work of suppressing violence and subversive activity was done by the Korean National Police and the Korean Constabulary.

Violence and subversive activities among the Koreans in the Kunsan area continued into 1947. There were fights, beatings of political activists, arson, and attacks on village officials and police. This was the situation that prevailed when I arrived in South Korea on January 5, 1947.

CHAPTER ONE

THE DECISION TO ENLIST

I turned eighteen in 1945, just after the end of World War II. As with most other young men at the time who were in their late teens, the prospect of being called into military service was very much on my mind. In fact, it was a frequent topic of conversation within the small group that I considered my best buddies. We were pre-engineering students attending the junior college in Santa Rosa, California.

By the spring of 1946, it became apparent that the draft was going to be continued despite the fact that the war was over. I had already received my draft card and was classified 1-A. Would the possibility of being drafted sometime during the summer months keep me from being rehired for my regular summer job as a member of a land surveying crew? Should I sign up for the fall semester in the hope that I would not drafted during the summer? Would I be able to complete my final year at junior college before being drafted? These were some of the serious questions that kept going through my mind in early 1946.

My buddies in Santa Rosa Junior College, Bill Brandt, George Doka, Parker Hall, and Bob Larson, were all of the same age and in the same draft situation. We all faced the same uncertainties, and talked about them often. Then one day one of us read an article in the local paper reporting that eligibility for the GI Bill would end October 5, 1946, even though the draft was to be continued. That spurred us into action. The prospect of not having the benefits of the GI Bill if we were drafted after October 5 made us realize how important the GI Bill would be to us. The five of us were not from rich families; we had to work during summers to help pay expenses. We wanted very much to go to a four-year college after graduation from junior college, but we also knew that we could not afford it. We were able to attend the local junior college because the fees were minimal, just a few dollars a semester, and because we lived at home and did not have to pay room and board.

We spent hours discussing our best plan of action. We decided that our wisest course would be to enlist in the military immediately, with a specified induction date that would fit our educational plans, rather than wait and be drafted at a time that might conflict with our plans.

We contacted the local recruiting office of each branch of service, army, navy, marines, to get the information we needed to make a decision. The navy and marines had much longer minimum enlistment periods than the army. The army provided enlistment periods of 3 years, 2 years, or 18 months. With a 3-year enlistment we could pick the branch of the army we wanted. The 2-year and 18-month enlistments gave us no choice — the army could place us anywhere.

The army recruiting officer explained that the GI Bill would provide for one year of college plus one month for each month of service. Thus, an 18-month enlistment would provide for 30 months of college. We calculated that if we returned to Santa Rosa Junior College after discharge to finish the second year of college using our own resources, the GI Bill would provide at least enough credits to cover the last two years at a four-year college. We were not pleased with the lack of choice of army branch with the 18-month enlistment, but decided that the shortest enlistment period was the best option for us. Our minds were made up. Then we approached our folks.

Parkers's father thought our decision was good, but his mother was opposed to the idea. Bob's parents were saddened by the thought of their son leaving home, but were otherwise neutral. They recognized that young men were still being drafted, and that enlisting rather than waiting was a rational decision. But the rest of us were not so lucky. Our folks were upset and opposed to our enlisting. They thought we should stay home and take our chances with the draft board.

Several days later, the five of us got together to talk about our situations. We respected our parents, and none of wished to defy them. Nevertheless, each one of us concluded that, for our situations, enlisting made sense. It was the only way we could be sure of paying for college. We also realized that at the age of eighteen we were at the time in life when we should take responsibility for our own decisions.

With the matter settled, the five of us went to the recruiting office and enlisted in the army. We were given a choice of induction dates. Bill, Parker, Bob, and I selected Tuesday, September 24, 1946. We decided that the sooner we started, the sooner we would be able to finish our 18 months and get back to school. I cannot recall why, but George was not able to go with us on the 24th so he picked a date a few days later. In any event, for the five of us the die was cast, the irrevocable decision had been made. We would spend the next year and a half in the army earning the GI Bill.

CHAPTER TWO

CAMP BEALE

Bill, Parker, Bob, and I left our home town of Santa Rosa, California, by Greyhound bus on the morning of September 23 and arrived in San Francisco in the early afternoon. We walked from the bus terminal to the Army Recruiting Center on Market Street. There we were instructed to report back to the center early the next morning when we would be sworn in and be given our orders. Then we were sent for our evening meal to a nearby Foster's Cafeteria, which was one of a chain of several cafeteria-style restaurants in San Francisco. Whenever my parents took my brother and me to San Francisco, we would eat at Foster's. That was always a great treat for me because the food was good, the portions were reasonable, and there were so many offerings to choose from. This time there was the extra bonus of not having to pay the bill.

After dinner we were put up at the YMCA. It was clean and comfortable, but I had trouble sleeping. I was not used to the clanking of streetcars and the roar of cars and trucks. Downtown San Francisco was very busy at night. Our house in Santa Rosa was on the edge of town surrounded by prune orchards where the nights were always very quiet. Also, I was probably overly excited about this new stage of my life that I was about to enter.

The next morning we went to Foster's for breakfast, again courtesy of the army, and then back to the center. At the center we found ourselves in a group of about 25 enlistees, some of whom we had grown up with. It was like old home week. In chatting with some of those in the group, it became apparent that most had enlisted for 18 months. I learned later that more than one million young people from throughout the United States had enlisted in the military in the late summer period prior to October 5, 1946, in order to qualify for the GI Bill.

The day began with our swearing in, after which we were given our orders. We were all being sent to Camp Beale, an army reception center about 40 miles northeast of the capitol city of Sacramento in the central valley of California, for processing and assignment. Now we were officially in the army.

We were transported as a group by bus. We left San Francisco about 4:00 PM and headed east over the Bay Bridge through Oakland, Walnut Creek, Concord, and then every small town along the highway in what seemed an interminable journey. There were no freeways in Northern California in 1946. The main highways were two-lane roads that went through the center of every town along the way.

It soon got dark, so I could not tell what towns we were passing through. To this day, I am not sure of the route we took, but it was a long one. Camp Beale was only about 150 miles northeast of San Francisco, but it took over 8 hours to make the trip.

We arrived at Camp Beale a little before midnight. As we got off the bus, we were lined up in alphabetical order and assigned to our barracks. It was at this point that Bill, Parker, Bob, and I were separated. I do not recall that we had any time together for the rest of our stay in the army.

The first morning at Camp Beale was an unusual, emotional experience for me. We were wakened abruptly at 5:30 AM by someone blowing a shrieking police whistle in the barracks and yelling, "OK you guys, hit the deck, up and at 'em." I was totally unaware of where I was. Everything was unfamiliar. The dawn light was barely visible. My usual sights and sounds of morning were suddenly different. I was confused, and my only thought was, "Where am I?" — probably not an unusual reaction for an 18-year old youth who had never been away from home and family before. Suddenly it hit me — "I'm in the army!" It was a strange, strange feeling.

Reality quickly returned when I jumped out of bed and began to dress. It was still somewhat dark and, for some reason, the lights in the barracks did not work. After making our beds in the semi-darkness, we were placed in line alphabetically and marched to the mess hall. That marked the beginning of 18 months of standing and marching in line. It also began 18 months of living in an olive drab world. It took quite a while to get used seeing everybody including oneself, dressed — and undressed — in shades of green.

Orientation began after breakfast. The first thing we learned was the great authority and importance of the bulletin board. It would specify by name where to report, what to wear, and any other instructions to be followed. The bulletin board had to be checked regularly each day. Failure to follow the instructions on the bulletin board would result in what was termed "severe disciplinary action."

Sometimes only two or three names would appear on the bulletin board, sometimes as many as 50. In the absence of instructions from the bulletin board, we were to follow the instructions given us by noncommissioned officers (corporals and sergeants) in charge of the barracks.

The bulletin board had an assistant to take care of the routine events of the day — the bugle. Its calls boomed from loudspeakers mounted outside on power poles around the camp. It told us when to get up, when to fall in line for chow, when to end the work day, and when to go to sleep. Our responses to bugle calls became sort of Pavlovian. Together with the bulletin board, the bugle and noncommissioned officers ruled our lives.

After several days we exchanged our civilian clothes for army clothes. At this time we were issued a burlap sack with an address label. We were told to stuff all our civilian clothes and shoes into the sack, put our home address on the label, and throw the sack into a bin for mailing. Then we proceeded down a long row of tables where, at each station, we were tossed some article of clothing or gear. The clothes we were issued were approximations of our sizes, usually on the generous side. In a letter home I wrote:

We got our clothes yesterday after standing in line about 2 hours. Everything fits me except my O.D. (olive drab) pants which are too long. They won't fix them for me and it's against the law to fix them yourself so I just roll them up. There are a lot of rookies around here that have been in about a week and their clothes are all too big. They remind me of the funny papers.

Now I was one of them. Newer arrivals probably had the same impression of me as I had of the fellows who arrived at Beale before me — a young guy marching around in clothes too big for him, like a character in the comic strips.

One of the first orders from the bulletin board was to fall out on the parade ground the next morning wearing only a raincoat, shoes, and fatigue hat — the uniform for physical examinations. My companions from the bulletin board and I were marched to the building where the physicals were given. All went well until we were lined up for shots. In my letter home later that day I wrote that I got a vaccination and two shots that were not as bad as I expected. I probably did get two shots, but I do not remember — I suffered the most embarrassing experience of passing out.

I came to while lying on the floor with someone patting me and saying that I'd be all right and to go get a drink of water. On looking around the area where I had been dragged, I saw that I had no cause for embarrassment. I was lying among several other bodies in various stages of consciousness. While we were languishing on the floor, the shot line was proceeding unconcerned and uncaring.

I wrote home that the food at Beale was good and there
was lots of it:

> The only trouble with eating around here is that you
> have to stand in the chow line for about $1/2$ an hour.
> They really give us a lot of butter here. They only
> give us one slice of bread, but we also get about $1/4$
> of a cube of butter to go with it.

Because butter had been difficult to get during the war,
it was a real treat for me. I just spread it on thick and
enjoyed it.

All recruits had to take a turn at KP before leaving Beale.
The bulletin board told us when our turn came. We were
told to tie a towel at the foot of our bed and the noncommissioned officer in charge of quarters during the night
would wake us at the appropriate time, about 3:30 in the
morning. KP started with the shock of being wakened out
of a sound sleep in the predawn darkness. The few of us
selected for the day dressed and headed over to the mess
hall. It was one of the few times I recall not marching in
line — there were too few of us and no one in authority
was around to give the order

At the mess hall, we reported to the person in charge of the
KP detail, commonly known as the KP pusher. He checked
off our names, gave us our assignments, and supervised us
closely. Assignments changed during the day as need dictated. We cracked eggs, peeled vegetables, opened cans,
stirred soup, served food, and so forth. But the really heavy
work came after each mealtime was over. Everything had
to be cleaned and scrubbed. Then food preparation began

again for the next meal. After dinner, not only pots, pans, food trays, and utensils were washed, but so was everything else in the mess hall. KP was over about 11:00 PM. We returned to the barracks tired, greasy, and thankful that the day was over.

KP opened my eyes to the wastefulness in so much of the army way of doing things. Our family was poor; thus, we did not have a lot of possessions. I was taught to respect and take care of the things I owned — clothes and toys and, as I grew older, tools, books, and other material things. Therefore, I was shocked at some of the KP procedures. Just the replacement of cutlery must have been a big budget item. We cleaned dirty trays by banging them on a wooden rail over a slop bucket. Everything left on the trays went into the garbage — knives, forks, and spoons along with food leftovers.

After several days of marching here and there, it dawned on me that the same fellow was always in front of me. This was logical because we marched everywhere in alphabetical order and his name began with M — William D. Mette. Mette and I got to be friends, but when we were assigned to different units in Korea, I thought our association had ended. However, we were to meet again in Korea and, when my tour of duty in Korea was over, who was in front of me in line on the troop ship going home? None other than my friend Mette.

Interestingly, many years later Mette and I met again by accident. My wife and had I stopped for lunch at the Nut Tree, a well-known tourist spot in Vacaville, California, and there was Mette and his wife sitting at an adjoining table.

After getting out of the service, he went to college and became a school teacher. It was a great pleasure visiting with him again.

After about ten days at Camp Beale, the bulletin board told a group of us to pack our things and fall out on the parade ground the next morning, October 3. We were to be transported to Fort Bliss, Texas, for basic training.

CHAPTER THREE

FORT BLISS

We left Camp Beale, California, about 5:30 PM on October 3, 1946, and traveled by troop train to Fort Bliss, Texas, via Los Angeles. It was an exciting experience because trains had held a great fascination for me for as long as I can remember. I grew up near the railroad tracks in Santa Rosa and spent many an after-school hour watching the locomotive engineers and maintenance crews attend the big steam locomotives. Some of the men took an interest in the little gawking kid who hung around the locomotive maintenance area. Sometimes they would let me climb up into a cab, sit on the engineer's seat, and pretend I was traveling full speed down the tracks.

The train that took us to Fort Bliss was a special train that waited for us on a side track at Camp Beale. The train was composed of two troop sleepers, six Pullmans, and an army kitchen car. We boarded the train alphabetically, in single file. As the train filled up, the Pullman berths were taken first and I ended up in a boxcar bunk. My first night was miserable:

I slept in a troop sleeper the first nite and got about 2 hours sleep. The reason I got such a little amount of sleep is because a troop sleeper is a boxcar with bunks in it. They are so rough to ride that there are safety belts running vertically along the bunks to keep the fellows from falling out of bed.

There also were heavy straps across the big sliding door, which was kept open during the whole trip. The big open door made the troop car pleasantly airy, though very noisy.

The next day we gathered around the boxcar doors to watch the passing scenery. Somewhere during this time I encountered Parker and learned from him that Bill had been sent to Fort Lewis. I did not see Parker again on the train or when we arrived at Fort Bliss. I finally located him after I wrote to my mother to ask his mother what his address was. The Santa Rosa mothers had a great network. Parker and I did not have much time to visit because we were kept so busy. Parker started his basic training a week earlier than I, so he left Fort Bliss a week before I did.

The train arrived in Los Angeles about noon and had a six-hour layover. All we saw of Los Angeles was the railroad station because the Colonel would not let anyone off the train. We mingled back and forth through boxcars and Pullmans while in the station.

Luckily, I met another recruit from the Pullman section who was fascinated by the boxcars and wanted to trade places with me. We checked with the first officer we found to see if it was all right to switch. He said he could not care less where we slept as long as it was on the train. That night I slept soundly in a Pullman berth. I never met up again with the fellow who traded places with me. I sure did not go looking for him.

From Los Angeles we traveled through the deserts of Arizona and New Mexico along the route that Interstate Highway 10 now follows. We arrived in El Paso about 7:00 PM on October 5 and were taken to Fort Bliss in army trucks. Upon arriving at the battery area, we were lined up in long rows four deep, given the rules of behavior, and assigned our quarters. We were told that we could not go anywhere outside of our battery area without supervision. Again we were advised to heed the all-important bulletin board located outside of the battery orderly room. It would inform us each day of what to wear, what our chores for the day would be, any special individual orders, when and where to go for sick call, and so forth.

Our quarters were in Logan Heights, a section of Fort Bliss that had been built during World War II. Logan Heights was an anti-aircraft artillery basic training center. In the artillery, a full-strength battery is made up of about 200 men (a battery in the artillery is equivalent to a company in the infantry). Because there were about 200 of us in the new arrival group, we were an appropriate number to form a battery. Thus, we became D (Dog) Battery.

Logan Heights had huts instead of barracks. The huts were little buildings made of wood and tar paper, about 15-feet square, arranged along short dirt streets. I was assigned to the second hut on one street. I liked the huts very much better than barracks because they were more home-like. Each hut accommodated five men. The four other fellows

in my hut were all about my age and had similar backgrounds, except they were all from different parts of the
west. There also was one fellow from Hawaii. The five of
us were happy that we finally had an address to send home
so family and friends could write to us.

The Sunday before the start of basic training I wrote home
to tell my folks about Fort Bliss and my roommates:

> Fort Bliss is situated in the hills above El Paso. From
> where I am now I can see a level plain as far as the
> horizon. In case it might be of interest to you, the
> elevation of El Paso is 3719 ft. above sea level.

> I guess you would like to know about the fellows I
> am living with. I'll start with the North East cor-
> ner of the hut and tell you what I know about them.

> Robert Bradley is lying on his cot reading the funny
> papers. He is close to 19 years old and hails from
> Santa Barbara, Calif. He just got out of high school
> and was a life guard at the beach this summer.

> Next is Maloye Warner, who right now is lying
> down writing a letter. He comes from Salt Lake
> City, Utah, and is really full of tall stories. We never
> know when to believe him. He is also close to 19.

> I come next. I think you know me all right.

> The east side of the hut has two more cots. Sleep-
> ing on one of them is Russell Pryor from Alameda,
> Calif. He is 20 years old. He enlisted just before he

got his induction papers. I don't understand how he passed his physical because he has to wear real thick glasses all the time. He can't see a thing without them.

Next is Walt Lum lying down reading a magazine. He is a civil engineer and graduated from Purdue University last Spring. He is Chinese and from Honolulu. He is by far the smartest in the hut. He uses perfect English and is a swell guy. He is 26 years old. He also enlisted when he got his induction papers. He was deferred all through the war.

Fort Bliss was my first experience with a highly structured military organization. It was a huge operation. It had a battalion size mess hall that must have accommodated at least 1000 people at a time. To ease the frustration of standing in chow lines, we were marched to the mess hall in battery-size groups of about 200. Each battery then waited in one place until its turn came to enter the mess hall.

We waited for over an hour at every meal before going to the chow line. Most of us did not stand the whole time. Some sat or laid down and took a nap, read a book, or just contemplated fate. One day while lying on the ground gazing at the sky, we saw, by chance, the vapor trail of a V-2 rocket that had been launched from White Sands, New Mexico. We knew it was a V-2 vapor trail because we had read that many V-2s were captured from the Germans at the end of World War II and taken to White Sands for study.

Usually, all I could think of as I waited for chow was what an awful job it must be for the fellows on KP. I knew I had that to look forward to. It happened more quickly than I thought. Two days after I arrived at Fort Bliss, the bulletin board told me to report for KP the next morning. The other fellows in my hut and the hut next door suffered the same fate. So, as did my companions, I tied my towel to the foot of my bed and was awakened in the early hours of the following morning. In a letter home I wrote:

> I and the rest of the fellows in the first two huts had KP yesterday for 17 hours — what a life. Two other fellows and I peeled 8 sacks of potatoes yesterday afternoon. We'll have KP only once more while we're here — that's one consolation.

The first week at Fort Bliss was sort of a preparation for basic training, which began the second Monday after our arrival. During the first week we were marched around a lot — for what purpose we could not quite figure out. We were issued more clothes and, one day early in the week, marched to the PX. where the barbers went to work on us, mercilessly chopping off our hair. A number of fellows who sported long Hollywood hairdos sure looked funny after their trip to the barbers.

During the first week we were also given aptitude and IQ tests. We were told to do our best on these examinations because they would determine what assignments we would get and our futures in the army. There were lots of rumors circulating around at this time about how we would be selected for various jobs and privileges, based on age, education, past experience, and so forth. But like most army rumors, they turned out not to be true. Apparently nothing mattered, not even aptitude or IQ scores, because everyone in my battery eventually received the same as-signment — the infantry. However, we were given the op-portunity to volunteer for some more dangerous assign-ments. For example, one afternoon a paratroop officer came to talk to us and tried to convince us to join the airborne infantry. I do not recall that he had any success.

I wrote often about the Texas weather because it was so different from what I knew in California. A progression of reports from October 8 to November 17 described the changes:

> The weather here is clear as a bell and comfortably warm in the daytime. The mornings are real cold and the nights are clear and cold. We all sleep with our long johns on, but they don't do much good. We start freezing about 4 AM. We already have 2 blankets and they're going to give us comforters one of these days. The weather is just right in the daytime.

> The weather is beautiful here. However, last night it rained, thundered, and lightninged. I guess you would call it an electric storm because the lightning looked like long jagged streaks.

> We had a wind and dust storm a couple of nights ago. The dust was like fog and the wind so strong you could hardly walk against it. A window in our hut was blown in about 3 in the morning and made a crash that woke us all up. I thought for a while that the wind was going to blow the whole hut away.

The weather is still hot here. I'm beginning to think winter will never set in around here.

The wind blew all day today, and consequently the dust was terrific, to put it mildly. This part of the country must be part of the famous dust bowl. I had to wash my ears twice today to keep them tolerably clean. That dust really is something.

The weather is still hot here but the sky is getting cloudier every day. I guess winter is finally coming.

The weather here has turned cold. So cold that it hailed today. It didn't rain though, so I didn't get wet. Everybody is wearing long Johns [sic] and sweaters under their fatigues and they're freezing anyway. We wear gloves in the morning because it is cold enough to make your hands numb. This dry cold around here really penetrates.

Basic training started on Monday, October 14. The routine for the next eight weeks, after the usual early morning chores and breakfast, was to fall in at 8:00 AM, march for an hour, have physical training for an hour, and spend the balance of the day in lectures, demonstrations, and field practice.

Basic training was conducted by World War II veterans who had chosen to stay in the army. They were a hard-nosed group of men, very serious, whose job it was to instill discipline in a mixed bag of mostly teenagers. They displayed no outward feelings of empathy or friendship for the recruits, which was understandable and probably for our own good, but at times we thought they went out of their way to frighten us.

One very vivid recollection I have of their scare tactics was on an overnight training mission in the desert. They stressed numerous times the day before that there were a lot of scorpions out there in the desert and that they lost three or four trainees to scorpion bites during every such mission. I was really frightened and worried about the night in the desert. None of us slept very well during that night, not just because of fear of scorpions; the desert was full of sticky, prickly plants, and a high wind blew a lot of sand around.

The wind actually provided a bit of comic relief for us. Each time we put up our pup tents, the wind would blow them down. It was frustrating, but eventually became laughable. The laughter helped relieve our tensions. When we finally succeeded in getting our tents up we hit the sack.

Some of the exercises and demonstrations were also designed to toughen us. I wrote to my father about one that was very uncomfortable:

> We had a demonstration of chemical grenades the other day. They set off three phosphorous grenades and smoke grenades of almost all colors. Then we topped everything off by going into a room filled with tear gas with our masks on. After we were in the room a while we had to take our masks off and say our name, rank, serial number and address before we could get out. That gas is really the stuff. It

makes your eyes and throat burn and you want to
get out of there as fast as you can.

On the second day of basic training we received our rifles.
They were 30-caliber M-1 rifles, also known as Garands.
They weighed about ten pounds and held eight rounds in
a clip. We were taught how to handle them safely, how to
clean them, take them apart, and put them back together.
The instructions we received for cleaning our rifles marked
the beginning of a skepticism that accompanied me
throughout my time in the army. I wrote to my father:

> We were taught how to clean our rifles the other
> day. I don't think it's a very good way, but that's
> the way they want it. The method is to take your
> rifle to the showers with you and scrub it with G.I.
> soap and water — believe it or not. They say there
> is the right way to do things, and the army way to
> do things. We do everything the army way.

Our instructor told us to listen carefully to him about how
to inspect our rifles, because if we did not learn from him,
the rifle would teach us by mashing our thumb. He called
this the M-1 thumb. To do the inspection, the breech area
was opened by pulling back the spring-loaded bolt and se-
curing it with the locking device. The problem occurred
when closing the bolt after inspection. The trick in avoiding an M-1 thumb was to keep the thumb out of the way
while releasing the powerful spring-loaded bolt as it
slammed closed. Every soldier who has ever used an M-1
rifle has quickly learned this trick. Fortunately, I always
got my thumb out of the way in time.

Our rifles became part of us. We were required to carry them with us everywhere, and before long felt out of place without them. We had been told that we were going to live with our rifles and that we had better get used to them. And so we did. We committed our rifle numbers to memory, because the army made these numbers as important in our lives as our names and serial numbers.

About two weeks before the end of basic training we were given an intensive week of practice on the rifle range. We were wakened each morning at 3:30 AM and marched to the mess hall. After chow we had 40 minutes to march four miles, with full pack and rifle, to the rifle range. We practiced all day until sundown with only a break for lunch, which was hauled in by truck from the mess hall.

The rifle range had a long row of what seemed like hundreds of bull's-eye targets. Each was six feet square and about 200 yards distant from low berms on which rifles were fired. Directly in front of the targets was a concrete trench about seven feet wide and seven feet deep. Half of us fired at the targets while the other half worked in the trench attending the targets. After each round, the targets were pulled down into the trench, scores recorded, holes marked so the riflemen on the berms could see how well (or poorly) they did. Finally, men in the trenches pasted over the holes and returned the targets to position.

Firing was very formalized, with orders given from a tower. There was a sergeant for every seven or eight men firing to make sure there was no horseplay. Everyone fired at the same time on command. After firing several rounds from different positions, such as down on the belly, sitting, kneeling on one knee, and standing, we exchanged places with the fellows in the trench.

We were told that selection for assignment to the infantry would depend on how good we were on the rifle range. There were three grades of competence. Out of a possible 210 points, a score of 180 or more was Expert, 165 to 180 was Sharpshooter, and 140 to 165 was Marksman. Anyone with a score below 140 did not qualify and had to keep trying until he did qualify. I do not know what happened to anyone who was unable to qualify. With regard to my score, I wrote to my family:

> I came out just about where I wanted to (just qualified — 158). I figured that if I got a good score I might get put in the infantry so I just scored high enough to get by.

I do not recall if that was the real reason, or that I just had no real pleasure in guns and just could not do better. The latter was the more probable. Regardless of whether I could do better or not, I do recall feeling very certain at the time that the way we were being trained just did not fit my way of learning.

In any event, our scores really did not matter, because we all went into the infantry anyway. Further evidence that our scores mattered little was the fact that, on leaving Fort Bliss, I found I had been rated as an anti-aircraft machine gunner, even though I had never seen an anti-aircraft weapon, much less fired one.

Almost all of the firing practice was with our rifles, but we had a few sessions with two automatic weapons. One was the M-2 carbine and the other the M-3, a light, collapsible submachine gun, called a grease gun, developed for the parachute troops. The latter was an intriguing instrument of ingenious design. As I recall, it had a metal barrel about 12 inches long with a collapsible stock made of very thick wire shaped to fit the shoulder. When the wire stock was collapsed, the gun could be held with two hands and fired from the hip. It shot 45-caliber pistol bullets in clips of about 30. It had very few moving parts. The bolt had a fixed firing pin. Upon firing, the force of the blast would push the bolt back and eject the spent cartridge. The spring-loaded bolt would immediately return and fire again.

I really enjoyed my practice with the grease gun, especially firing from the hip. It was great sport for an 18-year old:

> We were out on the machine gun and carbine range yesterday. In the morning we fired a .45-cal machine gun called a 'grease gun' or M-3. It shoots 400 rounds per minute. Weighs about 7 1/2 lbs. and is really easy to handle. I sure did have fun shooting that.

Soldiers who were familiar with the grease gun used to tell us that it was a gun that could be played like a violin. This was because the relatively slow 400 rounds per minute allowed time for a person experienced with the gun to move from target to target between bullets. This was much more efficient with ammunition than the carbine, which was really a spray gun. I had difficulty with the M-2:

This afternoon we went over to the carbine range where we fired the M-2. It is both a full automatic and semi-automatic. It's a little faster than the grease gun, to be exact it fires 750 rounds per minute. They are really hard to hold on target. I was firing at a target 6 ft. x 6 ft. from 1000 inches and after 3 shots come out of that gun it is impossible to hit the target. It climbs uncontrollably. Half the shots missed the target entirely.

The restriction to the battery area ended the Sunday after the start of basic training. There were three things I wanted to do once I was able to get passes. One was to go to El Paso and Mexico, the second was to climb the low mountain that could be seen west of the camp, and the third was to visit Carlsbad Caverns only 80 miles away.

I used my first pass to go to El Paso on October 20. I apparently was not impressed:

> I finally got a pass Sunday to go to El Paso. I don't think much of the town. In fact, I don't think I'll go into town again. The streets are narrow and come together at all angles. The sidewalks are overflowing with soldiers, and the weather is unbearably hot. There are shows and service clubs on the post that beat El Paso in every way.

I must have changed my mind, because a week later I wrote:

> A couple of us went to El Paso Sunday afternoon to see if we had passed up anything the first time we went in town. This time we went to the YMCA.

and looked it over. It is a nice place, but it is overly crowded. It has a gym, bowling alley, swimming pool, and a day room. I didn't stay because it was too crowded.

And two weeks later:

Pryor and I went to El Paso this afternoon. We walked as far as the International Bridge. This bridge crosses the Rio Grande River and connects the U.S. and Mexico. We could not cross it because the passes we get here are for the U.S. only. Maybe one of these days we will get a Juarez pass. I hope so because I would like to go to Mexico being that I'm this close. There was nothing else to do in town, so we came back to camp.

I never got to Mexico while at Fort Bliss, but I did fulfill my other two goals. I tackled the mountain west of camp the morning before my second trip to El Paso:

I climbed the mountain Sunday morning with Warner. He's a mountain climber from way back. I don't know the name of the peak, but it is in the Franklin Mts., if that clarifies the situation. It was quite a climb. We passed thru cactus and all kinds of thorny plants. The ground was dry as a bone. It got real steep toward the top and we had to go on our hands and knees.

There was a little three-cornered metal building at the top that had a beacon on top of it. The beacon used acetylene for fuel. I don't know how those

cylinders were ever carried up there. We scratched
our names on the building just like a thousand other
people did. The building was covered with names.
I looked for one from Santa Rosa, but didn't locate
any. The closest name I found on the building was
from Alameda. I don't remember the name now,
but I don't know him.

We didn't see any snakes or other living things on
the way up or down. However, on the way down I
slipped and fell, hind end first, on a small but very
spiny cactus. We pulled most of the spines out of
my rear end and upper legs immediately after I fell.
I still have some spines in me.

I later learned the cactus I had the misfortune to fall on
was a cholla cactus. The last of the spines came out, one-
by-one, over the next six months.

My trip to Carlsbad Caverns on November 3 was really
something to write home about:

It was quite a trip. We left El Paso at 8:15 this morning and arrived at the caverns at noon, just in time
for the next tour through.

I'm getting ahead of myself already. First I want to
tell you a little about the country we passed thru.
For the first 35 miles the land was rolling hills and
desert, like Nevada. Then we passed thru a salt
flat. It was pure white and flat as the law allows.
That flat was smoother than the highway.

Next we passed over the highest highway pass in Texas — 6600 ft. Right by the side of the highway was the highest peak in Texas. The elevation of the peak was a little over 10,000 ft. The rest of the trip was cattle country — sparse grass and sage brush.

Now to get back to the caves. The trip thru started at 12:15. For once in my life my uniform helped me out. The civilians had to pay $1.50 to get in the caverns and I got in <u>free</u>. Pretty sharp. We walked downhill until about 1:45. We were then 720 ft. underground and in a subterranean cafeteria. It could seat 1000 people. The thing that impressed me most was the monstrous size of the caves. It didn't even seem that we were underground. I thought Fort Bliss was a 'hole,' but I saw a bigger one today.

After we had eaten and rested, we walked around for another hour and then came back to the cafeteria. Then we went up the elevator to the surface. What a ride! 720 feet in 30 seconds. My ears really popped. We then went into a store by the cavern entrance and I bought the stuff you will receive in a couple of days.

I also got my name in the paper. White's City — that's 6 miles from the caverns — puts out a paper every day with the names and home towns of all the visitors. You will get it in the package I will send as soon as possible. Save the paper because I would like to keep it as a souvenir.

Our training cycle was completed on November 20. The next few days were spent getting ready for departure. Basic training had been very disciplined and demanding, but less difficult than I had anticipated. On the positive side, it had provided an opportunity to visit parts of the country I had never been to before, and I really enjoyed meeting so many other fellows with different backgrounds and different interests from all over the country.

I was amazed at how many there were among us who were well educated, both enlistees and draftees. In my hut alone all had at least one year of college. I was pleased, too, that all the fellows I met were really nice people. There were no bullies and none had chips on their shoulders.

While at Fort Bliss, I thought a great deal about the wisdom of my decision to enlist in the army. I shared my thoughts with my folks:

> I'll now give you my opinion of the draft situation. I'm glad I joined, because I think the draft will start again after the first of the year and I'd still be stuck. However, don't get the idea that I don't like it at home. I'd really like to be there now, but I've got to get this over with someday. I guess you've read that they're going to let out all the '45' draftees. Well, there are some of those around here and they're not getting out. I was talking to one kid who was still in after 23 months.

During our time in camp, we heard that there were a few young men who just could not cope with being away from home. I did not know any of them personally, but their situations made me sad. Some were enlistees and some draftees. They cried at night and would not take orders. They apparently could not stand the lonesomeness of being away from home and could not fulfill their commitment to the army. They were discipline problems for the army and were treated as such. Their punishment was to run for long distances with their rifles over their heads, dig ditches, and so forth. I have no idea what eventually happened to them.

Our battery was the last group to be trained at Logan Heights:

> We are the last cycle to be trained here as Logan Heights has been condemned by the 4th Army inspectors. After we leave, the AARTC [Anti-aircraft Artillery Replacement Training Center] is moving to Fort Ord, Calif. It is possible that we trainees will go there for more basic. I never know what's going to happen from one minute to the next.

Logan Heights was scheduled to be dismantled, not only because it was condemned, but probably more importantly, because the war was over and the extra facilities were no longer needed. Thus, Logan Heights began emptying out during our basic training period. By the time of our graduation ceremony there was only our battery left. We were told that after the ceremony our names would be called and we would be given individual copies of our orders. After that we were free to leave camp. We knew we would be going to Camp Stoneman, California, a port of embarkation, with a delay en route of a week or so. I was looking forward to going home for the interval.

Graduation was brief, with a few kind words and good wishes from our instructors. Then began the calling of names. One by one our ranks became fewer. Finally there were three of us left and there were no more orders! The sergeant left to go home, and panic set in. I could not believe it — the army lost me! We ran after the sergeant and asked him what to do. Logan Heights was now empty. We had no place to go. The sergeant suggested that we go over to the main part of Fort Bliss. He said they would put us up until it was decided what to do with us. The other two fellows left, but I refused to remain "lost." I persisted and, finally, in order to get rid of me, the sergeant and I went to the orderly room to look around. He found my missing orders in the top drawer of the desk, and I was on my way to Camp Stoneman.

Much later I learned that my persistence may have been the biggest mistake of my army career. The loss of my orders by the army put me out of the circle. The army would have found another slot for me, heaven knows where, but probably not where I eventually went. There was a saying around camp that there are only two places better than where you are now — where you have been and where you are going. Unfortunately, that did not hold true for me. My persistence resulted in my going to a place more unpleasant than Logan Heights.

CHAPTER FOUR

CAMP STONEMAN

I left Fort Bliss, Texas, on an army shuttle bus that went to the train depot in El Paso. Even though I had no reservations, I got a seat that evening on the Sunset Limited bound for Los Angeles. Because I was not due to report to Camp Stoneman, California, for about ten days, I decided to go home. On arrival in Los Angeles I went by a Santa Fe Trailways bus to San Francisco and then by Greyhound bus to Santa Rosa.

Needless to say, my mom was overjoyed at having her soldier boy home to fuss over and cook for. My brother Bob, who was six years my junior, seemed to have grown a lot in the few months I had been away from home. And my dad noted that I was still only a private. His observation that I had not yet been promoted reinforced his conviction that I should not have gone into the service. His disappointment in my lack of accomplishment was apparently assuaged when I reminded him of the benefits of the GI Bill. Despite his stern exterior, his manner indicated that he was really proud that his son was serving his country.

Parker, Bill, Bob, and George were all home about the same time. We got together several times to compare notes on our army experiences. We were all pretty satisfied with the way things were going. Everything was on course. Bob Larson and I were scheduled to go to Camp Stoneman, but Bob was due at Stoneman on a different day than I. The others were bound for Fort Lawton, Washington, and, ultimately, Japan. Bob Larson was also shipped to Japan.

The day finally arrived to say good-bye to family and friends and leave for Camp Stoneman. I left early for San Francisco where I caught a bus going directly to Camp Stoneman. The bus was crowded with other fellows like myself who had finished basic training and were reporting for further assignment. We arrived at Camp Stoneman in the early afternoon. MPs (military police) met us at the bus and sent us to a reception area where we turned in our orders. The reception area was a huge, roofed-over shed with three open sides and a dirt floor. It had a small office at one end where, upon turning in our orders, we were told to wait until our names were called.

My name was finally called about 10:30 PM. I joined other soldiers in a long line that was continually fed by new arrivals at the camp. The line snaked through the dark night from one building to another, with stops in each for various paperwork and medical procedures. Somewhere along the way we were reminded to check the bulletin board every day. It would give general orders for the day as well as any special individual orders.

At one station there was an inspection for venereal disease or, as it was referred to in vulgar army idiom, a pecker check. Venereal disease checks were common in the service and probably very necessary, but this time I was struck by the absurd picture of a medical corpsman sitting on a stool with a flashlight in hand looking at penis after penis in assembly line fashion. He surely must have suffered tremendous boredom in the process of becoming a world expert in male genital anatomy.

When we came to the station where shots were given, I was taken aback by the way it was done. The corpsman had a large syringe containing ten doses of whatever vaccine it was we were being given. He would pull a GI out of the line, give him a shot, and then hand the syringe to the GI with instructions to give a shot to each of the next nine fellows in line. Thus, every tenth GI became a "shooter." What struck me was how little respect this corpsmen must have had for us to turn such a serious procedure over to untrained servicemen. I considered it most irresponsible, but it never occurred to me to be concerned for my own health. I did not know at that time that the reuse of hypodermic needles could transmit disease from one person to another. I can imagine the uproar such a procedure would cause today!

We were finally directed to our barracks about 1:00 AM, totally exhausted. We slept in our clothes the first night or two because we had not yet been issued blankets. At 4:00 AM of the first morning the lights went on, whistles started blowing, and a voice boomed, "OK, come on, hit the deck." As we stood there in a half stupor, the voice boomed again, "You guys on the Marine Jumper get going, the rest of you back to bed." I did not know what ship I would be on — the bulletin board had not yet told me, so I knew it could not be the Marine Jumper. Looking back, I may have misremembered the ship's name. It may have been the Marine Dragon or the Marine Serpent. Regardless of which it was, some mishap befell the ship, and the fellows assigned to it returned to camp the same evening. However, I do not misremember the frustration the next morning when the scene of the previous morning was repeated. Again, we all jumped groggily to our feet at 4:00 AM only to be told shortly thereafter to go back to sleep.

The balance of the time at Camp Stoneman was spent doing routine duties and getting outfitted for overseas service. On the train going home from Fort Bliss, some soldiers who had been in the service for a while advised me to leave all of my GI clothes at home. They pointed out that Camp Stoneman was more than 500 miles from Fort Bliss and that we were entitled to lose all our clothes every 500 miles. In orientation, we had been told that the army would replace clothing rendered unusable by normal wear and tear, but if we lost our clothes or sold them, the cost of replacement would be taken out of our pay. I was still naive enough to believe everything I had been told in orientation. Thus, I brought everything I had been issued at Fort Bliss to Camp Stoneman.

The soldiers' advice turned out to be correct. At Camp Stoneman they issued what was called a model stock — everything we would need for our upcoming assignment — independent of what we had already been issued.

A day or two after arrival we were told to report to a certain building with all of our belongings. Inside the door we were told to empty our duffel bags and throw the contents on a big pile nearby. Then we moved in a line along rows of counters with our empty duffel bags. The bags were filled with new clothes as we went by each counter. At one place we received pants, the next shirts, and so on down through underwear and toiletries.

At each stop we were asked, "What size?" and then took what we got. When it came to shoes, I asked for 8D and got size 12! At this point I complained — no way could I wear size 12. I was told to shut up and trade them off in the barracks. Later, after a number of trades, I got a pair of 8 $\frac{1}{2}$ C which felt pretty good, so I stopped there. Everybody made trades of some sort. One fellow received an overcoat so big he could wrap it around himself twice.

Camp Stoneman was adjacent to Pittsburg, California, a small industrial town about 40 miles east of San Francisco. Pittsburg is located on an arm of the bay of San Francisco that leads to the Sacramento/San Joaquin River Delta. The area is very foggy in the wintertime, and so it was during my stay at Camp Stoneman.

During the day the fog was not much of a problem, but at night it was easy to get lost. The camp was a huge place that had served as a major port of embarkation for the Pacific Theater during World War II. All of the buildings looked alike on a dark and foggy night. Fortunately, the buildings were numbered. If we went out at night to the post exchange or some other place in camp, it was essential that we remember the number of our barracks building in order to find our way home.

During the six or seven days at Camp Stoneman, I pulled
KP once and guard duty once. My guard duty was from
10:00 PM to 2:00 AM on a foggy night at the Pittsburg dock
area. It was an awesome and moving experience for me.
There was an arch over the entry to the wharf that I was
guarding. It bore the inscription "Through this portal pass
the best damn soldiers in the world," or words to that effect. Alone, in the quiet darkness, as I walked my post, I
thought of the many thousands of young men who had
walked on the planks of this very wharf and who had gone
under that arch to the Pacific theater and never returned,
or returned as wounded veterans never to resume a normal life. My thoughts that night were very sad and sober-
ing. I had grown up during World War II, and had great
respect for all the people who fought in it.

Finally the day came when the bulletin board included my
name on the long list of servicemen scheduled to ship out
the next morning. We were to board the Eufaula Victory
bound for Jinsen. Jinsen? I had no idea where that was. I
had a pretty good knowledge of geography, but Jinsen was
new to me. At first I thought it might be in India. Then,
after checking around, I learned that Jinsen was the Japanese name for Inch'on, Korea.

From this point on there were no more familiar places and
few familiar faces.

CHAPTER FIVE

THE EUFAULA VICTORY

The afternoon before leaving Camp Stoneman to board the Eufaula Victory, the sergeant showed us how to pack. Certain things had to go into a backpack and others into a duffel bag. Our duffel bags would travel by truck to the ferry boat that would carry us to the Eufaula Victory. Our back packs would travel with us. After packing, we had nothing more to do but wait until we began our sea journey the next morning.

On December 23, our seventh day at sea, I wrote my first letter from the Eufaula Victory:

> The 16th of December we got up at 3:00 AM and went to chow. Then we marched two miles down to the dock [in Pittsburg, California] where we boarded a ferry boat. It was an ex-Key System ferry from San Francisco Bay called the Yerba Buena. The ferry left Pittsburg at 11:00 AM and took us to the Port of Oakland which is just south of the bridge approach [the San Francisco Bay Bridge] on the

Oakland side. We walked off the ferry onto the pier and from the pier into the Eufaula Victory.

While we were on the ferry, a young man approached a group of us to take orders for a picture of the Eufaula Victory suitable for framing. He was sure we would want a picture of the ship we were about to sail on. I ordered a picture, and then promptly forgot about it.

I was reminded of the picture about six months later in Camp Hillenmeyer. I received a letter from my mother saying that the post office had contacted her about a picture. She assumed I had been swindled through the mail, and had raised Cain with the post office. On August 3, 1947, I wrote a sheepish response:

> Yesterday I received that questionnaire that the post office sent you about that picture of the Eufaula Victory. I filled it out except for a couple of questions that you will have to fill out.
>
> When I was on the ferry boat on my way from Stoneman to Oakland I ordered the picture. The guy that was selling them said he was working for the army PX. He said the picture would cost about $2 C.O.D. I didn't pay him a cent. He didn't sell the pictures on the sly. He made a speech to the whole bunch of us and said he was working for the P.X. so I figured he wasn't a fraud.
>
> The reason I didn't tell you about it is that you would get mad as you told me not to buy any pictures from guys I didn't know.

I still have that picture of the Eufaula Victory, framed, on the wall over my desk in my study at home.

There were about 1100 of us on the ferry that took us to the Port of Oakland. From there we walked single file onto the deck of the Eufaula Victory. It was a cargo ship built during World War II that had been converted to a troop transport. It had three or four huge hatch covers, each with a small steel house built on top that contained a double stairway. The first men aboard went down the nearest hatchway to bunk compartments. Then as those bunks were filled, the line was sent down the next hatchway, and so on, until all of us were accommodated.

Each hold had a number of levels or decks, and each deck was divided into several compartments. In the sleeping compartments there were long rows of steel stanchions to which bunks were clipped side by side. The bunks were made of steel pipe frames about $6\,1/2$ feet long and 18 inches wide. Canvas sheets with metal eyelets all around the perimeter were lashed with rope to the frames. Each bunk was held in a horizontal position with chains running from the outer corners of the pipe frames to the stanchion. This enabled the bunks to be tipped up when more room was needed in the aisles.

Bunks ran from floor to ceiling with the bottom bunk about 4 inches from the floor and the top bunk just below the pipes that ran along the ceiling. I do not recall how many bunks there were from bottom to top, perhaps five or six, but the space between each was such that if you turned on your side your shoulder would hit the butt of the fellow above you.

When my turn came to go below, I went into a compartment about two levels down in the front section of the ship. When I saw how the bunks were arranged, I quickly realized that men in top bunks would have to climb on the lower bunks to reach their beds. I decided I did not want to be disturbed by people climbing up over me so, when the sergeant yelled, "OK guys, grab a bunk," I threw my duffel bag on a top bunk to claim it. It turned out to be a comfortable location despite the fact that I had to be careful not to hit my head on the pipes just above me.

As mentioned above, the Eufaula Victory was a cargo ship that had been converted to a troop carrier during World War II. It had a civilian crew employed by the Maritime Sea Transport Service, a government agency created to provide for the sea transport needs of the military services. It was a comfortable ship, 455 feet long and 62 feet wide, with a draw of 18 feet. It was powered by steam turbines and burned heavy fuel oil. The ship's average speed was 17 knots and it traveled about 425 miles a day. It was equipped to carry a passenger load of about 2000. Because there were only about 1700 of us aboard — 600 Air Corps personnel going on to Yokohama, Japan, plus the 1100 of us bound for Korea — the ship was not overcrowded.

In addition to sleeping quarters for troops, there was a mess hall and several large latrines in the central part of the ship. The ship had facilities for water conversion, but they were not adequate for a troop transport. Thus, there were huge tanks, centrally located, that held 834 tons of potable water to provide for cooking and drinking needs. Sea water was used for showers and for continual flushing of toilets and troughs used for urinals.

We started underway in early evening of December 16, 1946, and passed under the Golden Gate Bridge just before dark. People with queasy stomachs might find a description of the next few days at sea distasteful and unpleasant to read about but, because it was something almost universally experienced by soldiers who went overseas by troop transport in the service of their country, it should not be omitted or glossed over.

As soon as we left the dock, we were permitted to go on deck. I went up to the rear part of the main deck with several other GI's to watch the receding lights of San Francisco. Shortly after passing under the Golden Gate Bridge the ship began rolling on the ocean swells and the rigging began clanging (the crew had forgotten to fasten down the cargo ropes). About this time we began to notice a fine spray on our faces. We wondered why. Although the ship was rolling slightly, it seemed unlikely that it was sea spray because the sea was quite calm and the deck was high up off the surface of the water.

We leaned over the rail to look toward the forward deck of the ship and saw that many GI's were also leaning over the rail. Suddenly it dawned on us that they were seasick and their vomitus was being caught by the wind and spraying back on us. That ended the pleasure of the view of San Francisco. We decided to go below deck to our compartment.

Not too long after we went below, an apologetic voice announced over the public address system that there would be no supper that night because they forgot to put cooks aboard before departure. The voice also told us to watch the bulletin board for the names of those of us who would be recruited as "volunteer" cooks for the balance of the journey. Fortunately, they did not forget to load food on the ship. It was also fortunate that we had been given box lunches on the ferry boat that morning.

The first meal we had was breakfast the next morning — scrambled eggs with eggshells. The eggs must have been thrown whole into a food mixer. Actually, the amateur cooks learned fast and did a very good job. I remarked several times in letters home that our food during the journey was quite good and in plentiful supply.

If supper had been provided that first night, there probably would have been few diners. As the evening progressed the seas became heavier, and the roll and pitch of the ship increased considerably. Before long, almost everyone in our compartment became seasick. There was no relief from the steady and constant pitch and roll of the ship. The creaking noises of the ship were punctuated regularly all through the night with the sounds of retching.

Despite the discomfort of my compartment buddies, I slept fairly well that first night. My bunk ran parallel to the long axis of the ship. I found that by lying on my side I could stabilize my body against the roll of the ship. I still felt the pitch, but it did not seem to bother me as much as the roll.

I awoke early the next morning to an odd smell that suggested a mixture of rusty metal, oil, and sour vomitus. I looked down from my perch among the pipes and saw a puddle of vomitus about two or three inches thick rolling back and forth with the motion of the ship. I had not yet gotten sick, so I decided to dress and go up on deck for fresh air to avoid the possibility.

A sergeant was waiting on deck for live bodies to emerge from below to form a crew to clean latrines. I was collared as I stepped out and told to wait with a group of about twelve other GI's who apparently also had strong stomachs. I had been to a latrine and knew what a bad situation was awaiting us. There was vomitus everywhere and the urinals were overflowing from being clogged with solids that had been thrown up. I doubted that I could keep from getting sick if I had to face such a mess.

While we were waiting for the sergeant to complete his crew, a group of GI's came up on deck all at once. When the sergeant was distracted by the sudden appearance of so many able bodied men, I slipped away into the crowd and scooted on down to the mess hall. I felt no threat of punishment for my defection because by this time I knew that we all looked alike in our green fatigue clothing and that no one knew us individually by name, or knew who was where on the ship.

Surprisingly, there were quite a few people in the mess hall for breakfast that first morning. The eggshell-laden scrambled eggs and greasy bacon finally got to me. I knew I was going to throw up, so I ran up to the deck, leaned over the rail, and heaved up what little I had eaten. I did not get sick again during the rest of the journey, but a feeling of queasiness never left me until we finally reached land.

Mass seasickness ended by the time we were several days out of San Francisco. The sleeping quarters and latrines were all back in spic-and-span condition, and life settled down to a humdrum and monotonous routine. Despite the monotony, I rather enjoyed the voyage. The Eufaula Victory was a fairly comfortable ship, and the big, wide deck offered many pleasant places for relaxation.

We had two sit down meals a day — breakfast and dinner in the mess hall. At noon, KP's brought large metal garbage cans of soup to us on deck. We formed a chow line with our mess gear in hand. The soup was ladled into our cups as we passed by. Crackers, or bread, and apples were dispensed from boxes.

Between meals we had a lot of free time. We could use the mess hall to write letters, read, or just visit with shipmates. There was an ample supply of writing paper and books available aboard ship. I wrote many letters and read a great deal. I cannot recall the title of even one book, but I am sure none were very heavy reading. In addition, there were a lot of familiar faces and friends to visit with. Many of the fellows aboard had been at Fort Bliss with me. To top it off, a friend from my high school class in Santa Rosa, Eugene Pisenti, had a bunk just two away from mine. It was very comforting to have someone from my home town aboard ship with me.

The first shower I took after leaving San Francisco was surprisingly unpleasant. I described it a letter home:

> There isn't too much fresh water around so we have to wash and take showers with salt water. The tough part about that is you can't make any suds.

The soap won't even melt. It's like trying to wash
yourself with a piece of lard.

Even worse, after a sea water shower you felt sticky all over.
The last shower I took aboard ship was when we were in
the tropical seas of the South Pacific, near the island of
Guam. I decided then that because we were so near Korea
I would wait until we landed and had soft water for bathing before showering again. Little did I know then that I
would not be able to take what could legitimately be called
a shower for approximately seven more months.

The ship's paper, appropriately named the *Rock 'N' Roll*,
started publication at the end of the second day at sea. It
consisted of four or five letter-size mimeographed pages.
Every day it plotted the ship's position and gave its distance from San Francisco and from Guam. It included sum-
maries of important news events, national and international. It also had items about people and events aboard
ship, a column written by the ship's chaplain, a sports column, and announcements of various sorts.

The *Rock 'N' Roll* was our only source of factual information during the trip. We never saw commissioned officers,
and the only time we saw noncommissioned officers was
when they came among us to kidnap a crew to clean latrines. The public address system spoke to us three times a
day with a "Now hear this — fall out for chow." Communications from the bulletin board were primarily KP assignments. Aside from these impersonal contacts with the
people in charge of our lives, we were left pretty much to
our own devices and ignorant of our immediate futures.

We often likened ourselves to a bunch of cattle being transported from one place to another.

The weather began to warm after we were at sea four or five days and about a hundred miles north of the Hawaiian Islands. The days were very pleasant and the ocean fascinating. I knew the Pacific was a very large ocean, but I never fully appreciated how large until all I could see day after day was water and realized that there was no land in sight and there would be no land in sight for many more days. A joke aboard ship was that land was only a mile away — straight down.

I also never realized how large waves could be. There were huge swells that were as big as hills and valleys. As we plowed through the swells I could see that they were often more than half the length of the ship. The vastness of the ocean and the immenseness of the waves made me wonder about the thoughts and emotions of the early-day sailors who depended on the wind for power and took years to cross the Pacific.

One night, when we were caught in a bad storm, the ship pitched up and down violently with the huge waves. Every once in a while the ship would shudder and vibrate. I asked someone nearby what was happening, and was told it was caused by the ship's propeller coming up out of the water and spinning free.

During the voyage, I spent many hours gazing out to sea. Often I would lay myself down on the forward deck at the bow of the ship, where I could put my head out through the anchor chain hole and look down at the prow cutting through the waves 20 or 30 feet below. I was fascinated by the play of the waves, the flying fish, and the ever-present albatross. I could watch them for hours on end. The albatross came so close I could almost touch them:

> About 10 albatross followed us from San Francisco, and they are still flying along behind. I guess they will follow us all the way to Korea. They are great big birds with a wing span of 7 feet. They never flap their wings. They just glide around with the greatest of ease. They eat the garbage that gets thrown overboard.

> I also saw some more flying fish today. They are small, about 6 inches long, and look like those big insects with two wings — only they don't have wings. They come shooting out of the water and fly a few feet above the water for about 25 feet or so.

The ocean at night was equally fascinating. The one time I had KP duty was for an evening meal. Late that night I had the job of carting garbage cans up to the deck and tossing the slop overboard — I did not realize at the time that I was feeding the albatross. As the garbage went over the side, I noticed long waves of phosphorescence bubbling several feet out all along the side of the ship. I had heard about the phenomenon of light produced by microscopic marine organisms, but never had seen it before. I spent almost every warm night during the voyage peering over the rail to wonder at the fluorescent display, and then lying down on a hatch cover to gaze up at countless stars in the black sky.

Christmas day came as we crossed the international date line. The weather was so very warm it was hard to believe it was December. The ship was about 2800 miles from San Francisco and 2400 miles from Guam. We celebrated Christmas on December 26 because the 25th slipped off the calendar as we crossed the date line. We had not expected a celebration but, when the public address system told us to fall out for "dinner" instead of the usual "chow," we knew that something pleasant was about to happen. I described our Christmas celebration in a letter home:

> We had a good Christmas dinner, turkey and all that goes with it, but it sure didn't compare with your ravioli.

> We all received Christmas presents from the Red Cross and Salvation Army. The packages contained games (dominoes and checkers), candy, cigarettes, cigarette lighters, decks of cards, combs, and fingernail clippers. It was a nice surprise as I didn't expect anything.

As we approached Guam the weather became hotter and more humid:

> We're in the tropics now and it is hotter here in the winter than it is in Calif in the summer. All we do is sweat and drink water. It was so hot in the mess hall tonite that my clothes were wet all the way through. The butter was liquid. It has cooled off now as it is nite time. The breeze is really nice on deck. The only time it's hot is during the day.

Despite the comfortable temperature on deck, the heat in the compartments made sleep almost impossible. The only refuge was the deck, where there was always a slight breeze. A number of GI's took their blankets up on deck at night to sleep in the open air. I tried a couple of times, but could never get used to the hardness of the steel deck. By midnight I would wander down to my bunk.

The day before we docked at Guam we had a light morning rain:

> It rained a little this morning, but it stopped in about 1/2 hour and the sun came out. That produced one of the prettiest rainbows I have ever seen. The colors stood out real clear and it seemed to be real close to us.

As we approached Guam the next day, the public address system announced that the outline of the island could be seen on the horizon and that we would be in port for about 18 hours. We were told that we could not get off the ship, but not why we were stopping. We assumed it was to take on fresh water or other supplies. One positive consequence of the stop was that we were able to mail the letters we had written during the past few weeks at sea.

The weather was extremely hot and unpleasant. I decided to go below deck, down as far as I could below water level, to see if I could find a place where I could touch the hull to get some idea of the water temperature outside the hull. I found a place on the lowest level. The hull felt very warm — just the right temperature for a nice hot shower.

We docked in the harbor of Agaña, the capital of Guam. Although it was hot out on deck during the day, it was hotter down below. As a result, most of us stayed on deck and watched activities in the harbor while we were in port. Near shore we could see Quonset huts and other signs of military life. The beach was littered with all sorts of debris including many boats, some fairly large, in various stages of disrepair. Guam was liberated only about a year before we arrived, but it had also suffered a fairly severe typhoon a few weeks before we arrived. We did not know if the damage was a remnant of the war or the result of the typhoon.

Shortly before we left Guam, a large military tug headed our way, presumably to help push us away from the dock. We watched with interest, and mild disbelief, as it kept coming straight at us on a course perpendicular to the side of the ship. It did not slow down until it was too late. We could see the fellow in the pilot house suddenly pull the lever to signal the engine room for full reverse power. It did little good. The tug hit us broadside and put a large dent in the side of the ship above the water line. This seemed to be of no concern to people in charge. The tug pushed us away and we left the harbor under our own power, unharmed except for a few moments of consternation and a large dent on our right side.

After leaving Guam, the ship turned north, heading for Korea. The weather turned progressively colder — a welcome change from the oppressive heat of the tropics. The color of the sea changed from a brilliant clear blue to a more somber gray. The days were uneventful during this last leg of our journey.

In the middle of the night, several days after leaving Guam, a terrifying, crashing noise jolted me out of a sound sleep. I knew instantly that we had hit a reef, or another ship, or that some other terrible accident had befallen the ship! I grew up in a depression-era family that had believed that if anything bad could happen, it would. I assumed, before I boarded ship, that some disaster might befall the ship before it reached Korea. Thus, I slept with my clothes on, except when we were in the tropics, in order to be prepared for the eventuality. I had planned that my first action in the event of some emergency would be to make a beeline for the deck. So I did. I was met with two surprises.

The first surprise was that there had been no accident. Other GI's were on deck looking out into the darkness. The ship was stopped and there was no more rolling motion. I asked what had happened and was told we were in an outer harbor of Inch'on. Apparently that terrible noise that woke me was made by the dropping of the anchor. The loud, crashing noise was caused by the heavy steel chain being dragged violently out of its steel locker. The noise was ear-splitting in our compartment because it was in the front part of the ship near the anchor chain locker.

I had not heard this frightening sound before because we did not drop anchor when we arrived at Guam. Instead, we were pushed by a tugboat to a dock where we tied up. This was the first time the ship had dropped anchor since leaving San Francisco.

The second surprise was that there were about two inches of snow covering the deck. Overnight the weather had turned bitterly cold. We all stood around on deck shivering and peering out into the darkness, wondering what would happen next. Shortly before dawn the loudspeaker told us to pack our belongings. It also advised us to be sure to eat breakfast before leaving ship.

The Eufaula Victory had dropped anchor in the outer harbor, about six miles from the docks at Inch'on, because the Yellow Sea, including the inner harbor at Inch'on, had a 40-foot tide. Small boats rose and fell with the tide. In the harbor at high tide they were at dock level and at low tide they sat on the mud 40 feet below the dock. So great an excursion was untenable for large vessels such as our military transport.

Not long after sunrise we saw a military tug coming toward us towing a pontoon-like barge. It was a steel box about 20 feet wide and 30 feet long that apparently was to serve as a floating dock. After this dock was secured to the ship, a Jacob's ladder from the Eufaula Victory was folded out and lowered down to it.

The maneuver with the ladder was interesting to watch. When not in use, the Jacob's ladder was tilted up flat alongside the railing. When folded out from the railing and lowered, the treads formed a stairway about two feet wide. At the fixed, top end there was a landing platform. As the free end was lowered, the treads retained their horizontal position regardless of the slope downward. The ladder could be lowered alongside the ship or swiveled out perpendicular to the ship. As we watched these proceedings, with our duffel bags and backpacks by our side, we wondered how we were going to get from the ship to land.

The answer was not long in coming. In the distance we could see landing barges, called LSM's, approaching fast. They looked like big open shoe boxes with sides about four feet high and a flap at the front end. At this point we were told to pick up our gear and get in line. When the first LSM tied up to our floating dock, the line moved down the ladder and GI's jumped aboard. When the first LSM was filled, it turned toward shore and a second LSM took its place. I was in the third group off the ship.

When I jumped into the LSM I was surprised to see that the members of the small crew were soldiers. I had expected that such a vessel would be manned by navy personnel. I was also surprised to see how dirty, disheveled, and unkempt this crew was. Their clothes were worn out and had that hard shine that comes from ground in dirt. Their faces were grimy and unshaven. They looked like some of the hoboes that I saw, as a child, sleeping on the grounds of the railroad station in Santa Rosa during the Great Depression. I was shocked to see people in the military so apparently ill-cared for. I was soon to learn that this was the norm in Korea. Little did I know that I was seeing a reflection of how I would look in the not too distant future.

As I looked back on the ship from the beach at Inch'on, I wondered if I would ever see it again. It looked old, rusty, and battered. I thought that perhaps it would soon be scrapped. However, many years later, when my voyage on the Eufaula Victory was only a dim memory, I saw her again during a visit to the World War II reserve ship fleet in Suisun Bay, an arm of San Francisco Bay. In the mid-

1970's, in my work as an industrial hygienist for the State of California, I was asked to evaluate the hazard an infestation of black widow spiders presented to the workers who maintained the fleet. The names of all the ships in the fleet were listed on the wall of the fleet office, along with a map of their locations. One of the ships was the Eufaula Victory.

I asked if I could include the Eufaula Victory in my tour. Unfortunately, I could not because it was being painted. However, after my inspection of the spider problem, the supervisor who led me on the tour offered to take me to a transport of the same type as the Eufaula Victory. As we went below deck with miner's lights and wandered through the empty mess halls and sleeping compartments in the incredibly still darkness, many memories returned. I could almost hear the sounds of my friends and the thousands of men who preceded us as passengers on World War II troop transports. I could not help but think of the many young men who traveled these mothballed transports to the war in the Pacific decades before, many of whom made only a one-way trip.

CHAPTER SIX

YONGDUNGP'O

We arrived at Inch'on, Korea, on Sunday, January 5, 1947, after 20 days at sea. The ride from ship to shore was bleak and uncomfortable — the LSM was open to the weather. The day was gloomy and very cold with a gray, overcast sky and a brisk, wet wind. Where were we going? What was going to happen to us once we reached shore? All I knew was that I was with a crowd of young GI's who were, as I was, in the dark and being herded around doing what we were told. We did not know our destination was Yongdungp'o until we arrived there.

The LSM reached shore about 30 minutes after leaving the Eufaula Victory. The large ramp that formed the front wall of the craft was let down, and we made long jumps off onto the beach so as not to get our feet wet. Little did we know as we jumped off the ramp onto the beach, that in less than four years U.S. Marines would be landing on this same beach, under fire, in a war to drive out North Korean forces that had invaded South Korea and were in the process of occupying the entire Korean Peninsula.

It must have been high tide when we landed, because there were railroad tracks and a station just about 40 feet from the water's edge. The station was in a sad state of disrepair. It looked like an old ramshackle horse barn.

We walked to the station area and joined the groups from the Eufaula Victory that had arrived before us. There were sergeants among us who served as escorts to see that we made it to our destination. They told us to wait until the train came to take us to the "first repple depple," which someone finally translated for us as meaning the First Replacement Depot. We groaned when they also said that we would not have lunch, but would be fed when we got to the replacement depot. Now we knew why the loudspeaker aboard the Eufaula Victory was so insistent that we have breakfast before leaving the ship. Fortunately, the train was not long in coming. We climbed on board about 2:00 PM.

The train was made up of a steam locomotive and a long string of passenger cars. It was a troop train, but it had a Korean crew. The engineers wore fuzzy fur hats that made them look unlike any locomotive engineer I had ever seen before. Those big fuzzy hats made them look like wild men. I thought it would be fun to ride in the cab with them.

On the outside, the train looked like any passenger train one would see in the United States. There the resemblance ended. On the inside, most of the seats were missing and many of the windows were broken out. In numerous places there were holes in the floor where people had built small fires, presumably to keep warm. The missing seats probably had furnished the fuel for these fires.

The ride to the replacement depot took about two hours. It was a very cold, uncomfortable trip. We had duffel bags to sit on, but our clothing was not adequate to withstand freezing temperatures. Fortunately, the sights and smells we met during the trip were sufficiently interesting to distract me and turn my attention away from my discomfort.

For the greater part of the trip we rode through rice paddies and farmlands. There were several inches of snow on the ground. The beauty of the land was really impressive. However, a faint odor of raw sewage pervaded the whole countryside. The smell was evident even in the towns we passed through. Korea had no sewage system as we know it. We soon learned that human excrement was used as fertilizer in fields and rice paddies throughout Korea.

The small towns we passed through were so very different from anything I had ever seen before that I found it hard to believe my eyes. The streets were not paved, and the general air was that of poverty. All of the houses were one story, with mud-wood combination walls and thatched roofs. They had few windows, perhaps because the climate was too cold or perhaps because they were too poor to afford the luxury.

Along the tracks there were quite a few industrial buildings, none of which appeared operational. One of our escorts pointed out one abandoned building that had been a Japanese silk factory. The only functioning industries we saw were small electric power plants. The electric utility systems in the towns were primitive. There were no street lights, and the few houses that did have electricity had only one bare light globe hanging from the ceiling on a wire.

The train stopped at each station, perhaps three in all. No one got off or on the train. All space was taken by the thousand or so soldiers from the Eufaula Victory. The stops were probably made to take on water for the locomotive.

At each station we were met by beggars, mostly children. Few had shoes and their clothes were threadbare and patched all over. What was even more shocking was the sight of the little children. They wore only upper clothing (we later learned that diapering was an unknown concept in Korea in those days). The sight of little children naked from the waist down, toddling around barefoot in the snow, touched the hearts of everyone on board. We gave them money, candy, and other small items that we carried with us. Later, after a few short weeks in Korea, a cynicism set in among the GI's. Most of the Koreans we saw appeared to be reasonably well-fed. Thus, GI's began to feel that sending half-naked little children to beg from soldiers perhaps had been a way of taking advantage of softhearted Americans. Unfortunately, this cynicism eventually contributed to a cool and sometimes hostile relationship between the Koreans and the soldiers.

The Korea we were seeing from the train was probably little changed from the Korea of decades or possibly even centuries before except, perhaps, for modifications wrought by the Japanese, who had taken over the country at the turn of the century and occupied it until 1945. In sharp contrast to the primitive conditions in which the people lived, the railroad system was well designed and modern. The rail bed and tracks were in excellent condition and well maintained. The station buildings, although very run down and dirty, were of western design. They looked very much like railroad stations in the United States, with tile facades and concrete station platforms.

The contrast between the plight of the Korean people and the condition of the railroad system probably was a reflection of the lack of interest by the Japanese in their Korean subjects as opposed to their great interest in infrastructure. The Japanese efforts seemed to be directed toward military needs rather than human or societal concerns. However, I learned many years later, that the Japanese had greatly expanded primary education in Korea during their years of occupation. This probably accounted for the fact that all of the Koreans, peasant and professional, that I came in contact with during my service in Korea could read and write their own language.

In the transportation area, the Japanese developed systems that provided ease of movement of men and materials. Thus, the rail system had excellent road beds and block signals, but shabby rolling stock. They built solid bridges of concrete, yet all of the roads and streets we saw in towns and villages were unpaved.

The First Replacement Depot was near a Korean city named Yongdungp'o in a former Japanese military installation. The train stopped near the camp to let us off. Our escorts guided us to the parade ground where they had us line up in regular rows and columns, in no special order. There we waited an hour or more until the roll was called to see who was there and who was missing.

While we were waiting we were given the usual orientation, including the admonition to watch the bulletin board.

It would tell us when and where we would be assigned. It was stressed that the army was not going to hold our hands and lead us around. If we did not report as the bulletin board instructed, we would be considered AWOL and be court-martialed.

When roll call was finished, a sergeant walked along the rows, counting. At a certain point he extended his arm and said, "All men to my right, you're on guard duty. Follow this sergeant." Then he continued along the rows, again counting. The second group was assigned to KP. I was in the KP group.

We were marched to a former Japanese barracks building where we dropped our duffel bags and backpacks and then marched to the mess hall to eat. Our KP duty was to start at 2:00 AM, so after chow we returned to the barracks to wait. It was very cold, even inside the barracks. Many of the windows were broken and there was no heat. Each room of the barracks had a diesel stove, but there was no fuel. We passed the time talking and trying to sleep.

A little before 2:00 AM we were awakened and marched back to the mess hall. We entered a dark and dismal room that was very poorly lighted. It was the first stand-up mess hall I had ever seen. It had row after row of long narrow tables that stood about chest high. This had been the mess hall for Japanese troops.

We went to work immediately. My job was to break eggs for breakfast and cut stew meat for lunch. Memory of the first breakfast on the Eufaula Victory made me especially careful with the eggshells. The meat was a more difficult problem. It was boxed in big chunks, packaged and shipped frozen, and stored outdoors. I had to chop large blocks of frozen beef, first into big pieces and then stew-size pieces. Fortunately, I had worked in a butcher shop during my high school days, so I had learned how to cut meat without losing fingers.

At 5:00 AM we started to serve breakfast. The KP pusher told me to serve the canned grapefruit juice. Earlier that morning it had been poured into a large metal container on the counter. I had to stand on a stool so I could dip down with a ladle to serve the juice. As the mess hall doors opened I scurried up on the stool, ready to serve the first GI standing in line with his cup out. I dipped the ladle down quickly into the container and, instead of slipping into the juice, it hit with a clunk. The juice had a solid layer of ice on top. I quickly banged through the frozen surface and served some very cold grapefruit juice.

The cold not only affected the juice, but all of the other food we served:

> That was really a cold place. The bread was almost solid and the jam was like tar. They couldn't cut the butter so they used to give us $1/4$ of a pound at every meal. What a treat.

When breakfast was over and the mess hall had been cleaned up, we were marched back to our barracks. We were dead tired, but there was so much activity all around that sleep was impossible. So, a few of us who had become fairly well acquainted during the hours we worked together on KP sat in the barracks mulling over our situation. It became apparent to us that nobody knew us individually by name. We were just a group of bodies waiting for reassignment. We realized, too, that our duties while in the replacement depot would depend upon where we happened to be at the time some job or another needed doing — sort of a you-here-go-there basis.

The weather at Yongdungp'o was terribly cold:

> There are about 2 inches of snow on the ground now and the weather is cold. We all wear our overcoats now and appreciate them. As soon as we get to our outfits, they promise we'll get fur-lined parkas and heavy boots.

Little did we know that the promised parka and heavy boots were just that — only a promise.

The weather was too cold to sit around in the unheated barracks for very long, so two of my KP friends and I decided to investigate the camp. There were two inches of snow on the ground, the skies were gray, and the air was bitterly cold. The depot was set in a valley. We could see the surrounding hills in the distance, but the nearby terrain was shut off from view by a high fence.

In the camp there were about ten barracks buildings like the one in which we were housed, a large building that appeared to be an auditorium, and a few other smaller buildings scattered around. The barracks buildings, like all of the other buildings in the camp, were built by the Japanese for military use. They were very long, barn-like buildings with unpainted wood on the outside and plaster on the inside. The roofs were tile.

Each barracks building had a wide central hall with doors at both ends. The halls were wide enough for the troops to gather in formation indoors. On either side of the hall were a series of doors to rooms about 20-feet square that housed about 20 men. All of the doorways were only six feet high, which made for a lot of bumps on heads of taller soldiers.

Along the wall in each room there was a waist-high shelf about 30-inches wide made of beautiful natural-color hardwood, finished like an elegant oak floor. These shelves had served as beds for the Japanese soldiers. The center of the room was probably used for daytime activities such as reading, writing, or just relaxing. When the American military took over, the rooms were fitted with steel bunks.

We later learned from some of the men who had been at the depot for a while that the First Replacement Depot in Yongdungp'o was originally located in a former silk factory, probably the one that had been pointed out to us from the train. GI's waiting for reassignment slept on cots placed alongside machinery used in silk production. The depot was later moved several miles away to its present location, although the original depot in the silk factory was still used for overflow if two troop ships arrived in Inch'on at the same time. I regretted that I was not put up in the silk factory, or at least able to see the inside of it.

During our exploration we found a large pit privy, the first I had ever seen in the military. Over the pit was a wooden house, a four-holer with a urinal on one side, built on skids. When the pit was filled, the house was dragged over a freshly dug pit.

We looked, but found no evidence of a place to wash or shower. Even if we did find a shower room, it probably would have been unusable because the world of the replacement depot was frozen solid. We also looked for a post exchange, but did not find one. We finally concluded that a shower room and post exchange were probably in existence somewhere in the camp, but were for use only by the permanent residents and off limits to the large numbers of transients who went through the camp.

We went into the auditorium building that we had seen earlier in the day and found a day room that must have been operated by the USO, Red Cross, or some other civilian service organization. It was a very welcome change from all we had experienced thus far since landing on Korean shores. The room was large and warm. It was furnished with chairs and tables, writing materials, magazines, and paperback books. It also had an all-important bulletin board. We stayed long enough in the day room to warm our bones and to ponder the significance of finding a refuge from sergeants seeking involuntary volunteers for nasty jobs.

After leaving the day room we explored a few barracks buildings, several of which were uninhabited. All of the barracks were built on the same plan, a wide central hall running the length of the building, with doors on both sides that gave entrance to smaller rooms with the handsome sleeping ledges around their perimeters.

In one building we found a room where mattresses were stored. Mattresses were stacked floor to ceiling with little alleyways running in maze-like fashion around the stacks. That room filled with surplus mattresses made us think about how much more warm and comfortable our bunks would be with an extra mattress between us and the cold floor.

We wandered back to our barracks to make sure we would not miss the march to dinner. We found our return unnecessary because we were on our own with regard to meals. A bugle call announced the opening of the mess hall three times a days, and it was first come first served. The only time we were marched around was when it was to go as a group to KP or some other duty.

While waiting for mess call, a few GI's who had arrived at the depot two days before we did confirmed our suspicion that the best survival tactic was to keep on the move and keep out of sight. The depot administrators must have also known this, because a sergeant was almost constantly present in every barracks room. Even the most savvy and mobile GI was faced with finding a bunk each night, which brought him back under the vigilant eye and control of a sergeant.

As I sat on my bunk staring vacantly at our sergeant-guard, my thoughts went to the sergeant-free room filled almost to the ceiling with surplus mattresses. My KP buddies must have had similar thoughts. We were concerned that we were going to be tapped for KP again that night, so we decided to escape to the comfort of the mattress room at the first opportunity.

We did not have long to wait. Prompted by many complaints about the lack of heat in the barracks, our sergeant went out in search of some fuel. As soon as he left, we grabbed our duffel bags and backpacks and took off for the mattress room. Once there, we rearranged some mattresses to form a small room and barricaded the aisles leading to it. Then we made beds of mattresses piled knee high on the floor with a mattress or two for blankets.

We spent that night and the next in the comfort of our mattress room. We had no fear of anyone stealing our duffel bags while we were there as we did when we were in the barracks. We spent the days moving about the depot with periodic rests in the warmth of the day room. The people who ran the day room were very pleasant and kind to us. They were American civilians, quite possibly volunteers. I never did find out what organization they were with. I admired them very much for the hardships they must have suffered to serve the men in the military.

While in the day room we talked, and read, and visited the bulletin board. I found I was not alone in wondering about the mentality of the army. Most of the young men I was with were part of over a million who had enlisted in order to be eligible for the GI Bill during the last few weeks before it expired. Thus, we were a self-selected group of high school graduates who wanted a college education. Many of us had a year or more of college.

As a group, we were curious young adults who thought a great deal about many things. Our first impression of the army was that it was, for want of a more descriptive term, "Mickey Mouse." There was an almost total lack of communication between the people in charge and the enlistees about the what, where, and why of our tour of duty. Many of us were very concerned that we were not trained adequately. We had no idea of what to do in the event of war. That was a frightening idea because we knew how tenuous relations were between North Korea and South Korea.

The conditions we had found thus far in our short time in Korea gave us the impression that the army was an organization not serious about anything. The GI's who had been in Korea any length of time were dirty and unkempt. Their condition was not from want of self-respect, but for lack of facilities. Yet the occupation army had been in Korea for at least a year. The utter disrespect for costs, as exemplified by the total lack of concern if our clothes and equipment were what was euphemistically called "lost" every 500 miles, was mind-boggling to young men who had to scrimp and save in civilian life to by a pair of jeans or a shirt.

Probably the most distressing thing was being assigned to places and duties at random without regard to how we could best serve. We all felt we had some experience that could be of value to whatever our mission was. Because many of us who enlisted for the GI Bill were from families who could not afford much, we had to earn money as soon as we were old enough to work. We had skills obtained from jobs worked during summers and after school. Our individual abilities were ignored. We were becoming disillusioned.

On January 8, a notice directed to those individuals being assigned to the 63rd Infantry Regiment, 6th Division, appeared on the bulletin board. They were to report to the parade ground at 6:00 AM, January 9. There followed a long list of about 75 to 80 names, including mine and my KP buddies. Now we knew we were in the 63rd Infantry Regiment. We also learned that the shoulder patch of the 6th Division was a six-pointed red star. I wrote to my family about my assignment:

> Well, I finally arrived in Korea, but I haven't stopped traveling yet. I think I'm going to South Korea or wherever the 6th Division is. You guessed it, most of us are going to the infantry. I am going to the 63rd Reg. with quite a few guys that I know. A few of the fellows were lucky and are being sent to the MP's and QM corps.
>
> There's a rumor that the 6th is moving to Hawaii in about 3 months so maybe I won't be bad off after all.

Despite the fact that army rumors usually proved false, I felt hopeful.

After reading our names on the bulletin board, we decided that we had better go back to our barracks bunks that night. We were concerned that we would oversleep the next morning if we did not have the barracks wake-up call. That night we sure missed our mattresses.

CHAPTER SEVEN

TO KUNSAN

We left the First Replacement Depot at Yongdungp'o on January 9, 1947, at 7:00 AM. We rode in open trucks about six miles to a train station in Yongdungp'o. The station seemed to be a different one than the one we arrived at several days earlier. However, there was no doubt that the train was very different from the one on which we arrived. It was a mixed train, with regular passenger cars for the local population and troop cars for the military. The cars were clean, the windows were intact, and all cars had seats.

The cars were old, perhaps 1920-1930 vintage, and well-worn. They were also unheated and, thus, very cold. The engine was a coal-burning, steam locomotive, with engineers that wore those fuzzy fur hats that I had first seen on the train several days earlier.

While standing on the platform, I noticed that the locomotive had no headlight or bell. It had only a whistle. I learned later that the absence of a headlight and bell on trains was common in Korea. This was so different from trains in the

United States that it made me wonder. Korean trains ran as often at night as in the daytime. How could a dark and silent train avoid killing animals, or even people, who had little warning of a train's approach?

As I had noted on the train to Yongdungp'o, the roadbed was exceptionally smooth. The stations along the way were all of a similar art deco architecture, well built but in disrepair. The train made many stops along the way. The passenger cars, carrying Korean people, were extremely full. People stood crowded together in the aisles and vestibules, and even stood on the train steps.

Such crowding was apparently the rule rather than the exception. Korean passengers carried ropes with them so they could tie themselves to the grab irons on the door frames in the event they had to stand on the steps. The rope was tied to the grab iron on one side of the door, passed around the person's back so as to form a backstop, and then tied to the grab iron on the opposite side. Thus, passengers could stand on the lowest steps without falling or being pushed off the train by the movements of the people in front of them.

At every stop we were met by crowds of begging children. Fortunately, we had been permitted to bring with us all the C rations we could carry. They contained hardtack, candy, cigarettes, and tins of corned beef hash. At each stop, we opened some C rations and tossed the contents to the waiting children, much to their apparent delight. They laughed and scrambled, especially after the candy. The older children went after the cigarettes, valuable items they could sell.

The train followed a tortuous route through rice paddies, around hills, and through valleys. The hills were perhaps 2000 to 3000 feet above the valley floors. They were snow covered with small sparse conifers poking through their white blankets. We saw no modern structures along the way, even in the towns. The houses were the typical mud-wall huts with thatched roofs. The largest buildings we saw were the railroad stations. The scenery along the trip was beautiful, but the usual faint smell of raw sewage filled the air throughout the whole countryside.

About 5:00 PM, the train stopped in a town named Iri, about 150 miles south of Yongdungp'o — our starting point that morning. As usual, because we did not know where we were going, we just kept our seats. Our army experience had taught us that the wisest course was to just sit until we were told what to do. After quite a wait, it seemed as though the train must have reached the end of the line.

While sitting in our seats, we began to hear distant American voices from other parts of the train. As the voices became louder and more numerous, we could hear repeated questions and answers, "Is this where we get get off?," "This is where we get off," over and over. I remember shouting out, "Is this another rumor?" Then GIs began hopping off the train. I decided I had better follow. Then the train started moving. I began to have second thoughts, but as the train pulled out of the station, GI's kept jumping off. They walked along the tracks back to the station. We stood there wondering if we had done the right thing.

After what seemed an eternity, a sergeant who appeared to know what he was doing approached us. There were about

75 to 80 of us milling around on the platform. He told us to go to a covered shed at the north end of the platform and wait. He said someone would come to pick us up soon, and then he left. That was the last we saw of him.

It gradually got dark, and after about two or three hours, to add to our misery, it began to rain and snow. I could not believe what was happening. We were tired, cold, and hungry. Our C rations had all been given away, and there seemed to be no alternative except to stand in the cold and wait.

At last, to our immeasurable relief, we heard the roar of engines in the distance. Then headlights came into view. Army trucks had finally arrived to take us somewhere. The trucks that arrived for us were two-and-a-half-ton army trucks, also called six-by-sixes. They had canvas tops like Conestoga wagons and each pulled a 2-wheel trailer. I wondered at the time, in the back of my mind, why the trucks were so noisy, but did not discover the reason until some months later. At the time, I was too relieved at our rescue to concern myself with such trivial matters.

That night was such a miserable experience I still remember it and the thoughts that ran through my head as clearly as if it were yesterday. As the bunch of us rushed from the shed toward the trucks through the rain and sleet, I noted that there were six or seven trucks, all with canvas covers except one. "Avoid that one," I thought. Then I saw the trailers. As I ran by, I found that the trailers of the closest trucks were nearly filled with duffel bags. "Get to an empty one so my bag will be on the bottom and protected from the rain," I told myself. I came to a covered truck with an empty trailer and, without further deliberation, threw my duffel bag in the trailer and jumped in the back of the truck.

We sat on narrow benches facing the center, about 10 or 12 to a truck. I was thankful to be under cover and out of the rain and sleet, but little did I know at the time how much more thankful I would be later that I had pitched my duffel bag into an empty trailer.

After the trucks were loaded, we roared off on the bumpiest road I have ever been on in my life. The drivers drove as fast as they could and seemed to have no interest in avoiding potholes. It was a really terrible ride. In the headlights of the truck behind us we could see duffel bags flying straight up in the air and bouncing out in the dark. We pounded furiously on the cab to no avail. There was no reaction at all from the drivers. They just drove on as duffel bags continued to bounce out of the trailer.

We could see nothing of the surrounding countryside in the dark. We had no idea where we were, but from the number of turns we made and the constant shifting of gears, I assumed we were climbing somewhere on a mountain road.

A short time later our truck left the convoy and stopped at what we later learned was the 6th Engineer's motor pool somewhere near a city called Kunsan. The area was very muddy. The guard at the gate looked bedraggled and cold, wet and dirty. He was dressed in cotton clothes and looked soaked to the skin. What was really unusual was the way he carried his rifle. It was slung over his shoulder with the barrel pointing down. I had never seen a rifle carried that way before, but it became a familiar sight in Korea. Rifles were carried barrel down in rainy weather to keep the barrel dry.

Something must have been wrong with our truck because we were transferred to another truck, an army ton-and-a-half truck known throughout the military as a gutless wonder. This was because it had a 6-cylinder Dodge engine in a truck that was too big for the engine. The truck may have been too big for its engine, but it was not big enough for our group. We were much more crowded, but happy that we still had a canvas cover over us to keep us dry. As we climbed into our new vehicle, we were told not to worry about our duffel bags. Those that were not lost would be delivered the next day.

Back on the road the shifting of gears and churning of the engine increased. The truck labored so hard that it seemed as though the driver would have had to shift to second gear even to go over a mole hill. I was more convinced than ever that the road we were on was in some steep mountain terrain.

There were no trucks behind us now. Without their headlights it seemed darker than ever. After about twenty minutes the truck suddenly skidded and the front end dropped down. The drivers got out and so did a few of the fellows in the back with us. Because it seemed as though we would not be moving for a time, I decided to get out to look around at the mountains we were in. That was the first time I had seen the drivers. They did not speak to us and seemed scornful and resentful. It was obvious they could not care less about questions we had.

When I jumped down from the truck, instead of a mountain road, I found we were on a dirt road on top of a sea wall. The truck had slipped on ice and the front end had gone off the sea wall. Fortunately, it did not go all the way off the wall. About 12 feet below the road was the Yellow Sea. The tide was out, exposing a muddy beach. There were rice paddies on the other side of the sea wall. Again we were told to wait, but this time it was in the rain.

As we waited, the rain turned to a wispy snow. About an hour later a truck finally came to pick us up. This time it was a three-quarter-ton truck. Now we were really crowded. We filled the benches, the floor, and the cab. But again, thankfully, we had a canvas cover.

We were on the road again. It was approaching midnight, and my bladder was beginning to nag me. Many hours had passed since I had been to a latrine. When we finally went through a guard gate and came to a stop, I was desperate. An authority-type stuck his head in the back of the truck and said, "OK, five guys get out here." In a matter of milliseconds I went through a critical decision process. I had learned never to volunteer because I knew whatever it was it would be a dirty job. Also, I was in the middle of the truck so I knew that, in the absence of volunteers, I would not have been selected. But my body ruled and, in a blink, I clambered over everyone and shot out of the truck. As I jumped to the ground, I went up to my ankles in mud. My senses returned and I said to myself, "Boy, I really did it this time!" However, my bladder had given me no choice.

We were told to go to a nearby Quonset hut where we were expected. After a dash to the latrine and welcome relief, I came back to meet the occupants of the hut. They greeted us warmly and peppered us with questions about where we had come from, how long we had been in the service, what was the latest news from the States, and so forth. They were hungry for news.

After we answered all the questions they threw at us, we turned the tables on our new buddies and plied them with questions. We learned that we were in Camp Hillenmeyer, just outside of Kunsan, and that we had volunteered for the wire (communications) platoon of the Headquarters Company, 3rd Battalion, 63rd Infantry Regiment. They said they were so very glad to see us because we were among the first replacements they had in a year. They also said the camp was so short-handed they had to pull almost constant guard duty to secure the camp.

The wire company fellows told us how fortunate we were to have gotten off the truck when we did. They said the others in the truck that brought us here were headed for the 3rd Battalion's infantry line companies, where life was really miserable. Their days would be occupied with guard duty throughout the camp and in the town of Kunsan, marching and hiking, and doing all sorts of other dirty jobs. Their lives would be spent carrying heavy equipment such as rifles or mortars and machine guns.

By a lucky quirk of fate, I landed in a headquarters company. I gave silent thanks that I had been driven by a bodily need to volunteer when I did.

CHAPTER EIGHT

CAMP HILLENMEYER

After basic training, I spent the whole of my army career, January 1947, through February 1948, in South Korea at Camp Hillenmeyer. The site of Camp Hillenmeyer was a former Japanese military air base that was occupied by the 3rd Battalion of the 63rd Infantry Regiment shortly after it landed in Korea in October of 1945. The camp was located on the shore of the Yellow Sea about 10 miles southwest of Kunsan, a small harbor city (see map next page).

While I was in Korea, I heard that Camp Hillenmeyer had been named in honor of an army officer killed in the line of duty sometime earlier. However, no one seemed to know who this person was or the circumstances of his death. While writing this book, I sought information about Officer Hillenmeyer. The army seems to have no record of an officer named Hillenmeyer, or why the camp had that name. The United States Army Center of Military History has only a few records that mention Camp Hillenmeyer. These records indicate the following: The camp was formerly a Japanese air field known as Kunsan Airdrome; the site was

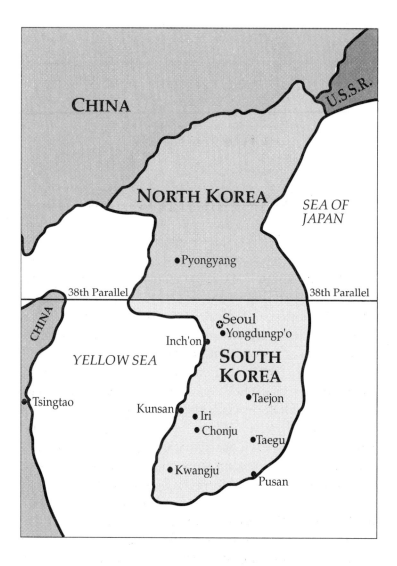

originally named Camp Iri by the United States Army; it was redesignated as Camp Kunsan in 1947; the site was also known as Camp Hillenmeyer circa 1947; and it was discontinued as an American military installation on June 16, 1950. I concluded that the reason for the name Camp Hillenmeyer was lost to written history.

Hillenmeyer would probably have remained a mystery forever except for one soldier, Russ McLogan, a member of Company K, 63rd Infantry, who heard a large explosion on November 30, 1945. Years later, while writing a book about his experiences as a young soldier, McLogan took the time to research and document the details of that explosion. He contacted the man who was his battalion commander at the time, and learned that on the day of the explosion, Captain Hillenmeyer, a staff officer in the 3rd Battalion, 63rd Infantry, was supervising the cleanup of a Japanese ammunition dump. Somehow a fire started and the large explosion followed, killing Captain Hillenmeyer, another officer, and many Koreans, and injuring several enlisted men. McLogan's book includes much more interesting information about the incident and the activities of the 63rd Infantry in 1945 and 1946 (McLogan, Chapter 13).

There were two American infantry divisions in Korea when I arrived. The 7th Infantry Division was arrayed near the 38th parallel, and served to guard this frontier against intrusion from the Communist north. It also served as an occupation force in the area near the parallel.

The 6th Infantry Division, comprised of the 1st Infantry Regiment at Taegu, the 20th Infantry Regiment at Kwangju, and the 63rd Infantry Regiment at Kunsan, occupied the

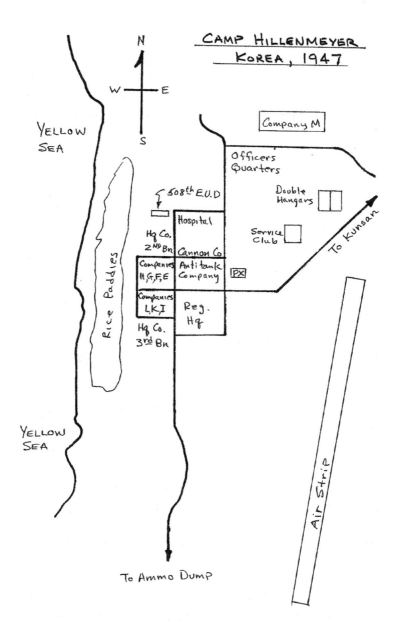

rest of South Korea. While there were other small American groups in Korea at that time, such as military government units, military advisors to the Korean Constabulary, and 24th Corps headquarters personnel in Seoul, the 6th and the 7th Infantry Divisions accounted for most of the United States military forces in Korea.

At full strength, a regiment such as the 63rd Infantry would have about 2500 men, but this number varied widely while I was in Korea. When I first arrived in early 1947, the 63rd Infantry Regiment had fewer than 1000. By early spring of that year, the regiment was at full strength. A large drop in manpower occurred a few months later when the army released all of its draftees. Troop strength continued to fall. When I left in early 1948, there were about 400 men in the regiment.

Each regiment of the 6th Infantry Division had three battalions. The 1st Battalion of the 63rd Infantry Regiment was stationed in Chonju, about 40 miles east of Kunsan via a dirt road. The 2nd and 3rd Battalions were stationed near Kunsan at Camp Hillenmeyer, the regimental headquarters. These infantry battalions were each made up of five companies; three rifle companies, a heavy weapons company, and a headquarters company.

The three rifle companies in the 2nd Battalion were E, F, and G Companies. The three rifle companies in the 3rd Battalion were I, K, and L Companies. The soldiers in these six companies carried M-1 rifles, except that about one soldier in ten was assigned to carry a Browning automatic rifle, more commonly known as a BAR. The heavy weapons company in the 2nd Battalion was H Company, and in the

3rd Battalion, M Company. In addition to rifles, their weapons were mortars and machine guns.

The companies of each battalion were divided into three or four platoons, depending on availability of manpower, each with like responsibilities. These were called the first platoon, second platoon, and so on. The headquarters company of each battalion was also divided into platoons, but each platoon in the headquarters company had a different function and was not identified by number. Headquarters companies included an antitank platoon, an ammunition and pioneer (scout) platoon, a wire (communications) platoon, and a medical platoon. In addition to platoons, each company had its own mess hall, an orderly room, and a supply room. All of these buildings were Quonset huts.

Camp Hillenmeyer was situated a few miles south and west of Kunsan, within walking distance of a beach on the Yellow Sea. I spent many hours of my free time walking on the beach. It was not beautiful, but it was quiet. I started exploring the beach shortly after I arrived in camp. My first mention of visits to the beach was in a letter home on February 10:

> I think I'll take a walk out along the beach this afternoon. The Japanese had a lot of gun emplacements and fortifications out there. I'd like to look them over. A couple of other guys will go with me and we'll take some pictures if it doesn't start snowing again.

The beach was interesting because of the approximate 40-foot difference between high and low tides. At high tide, the beach looked like every other beach I had ever seen, with small waves lapping at the shoreline. At low tide, the area was an impassable mud flat with the beach a mile or more away.

Several miles south of the camp was an ammunition dump, and a little beyond that was a rock quarry. To the west of camp, flat ground and rice paddies covered the strip about one-half mile wide between the camp and the Yellow Sea. Northwest of camp, overlooking the Yellow Sea, was a small mountain called Blacktop. In early April, I described Blacktop to my parents:

> I climbed a mountain yesterday afternoon with two other guys — Kennedy from Tenn. and Souden from Penn. It's the highest mountain around and used to be a Japanese fortification. From the top of it we could see Kunsan Harbor and the coastline as far as the eye would reach. It has caves and foxholes all over it. The caves were dug out of rock and only about 20 ft. deep.

North of camp, beginning at Blacktop and following the sea wall northward toward Kunsan, were rice paddies. In fact, from the top of Blacktop Mountain, one could see rice paddies occupying every flat area of the surrounding countryside. Small villages, accessible only by narrow paths, were scattered among the rice paddies.

Camp Hillenmeyer, as mentioned earlier, was located on the site of a former Japanese air base. The dirt air strip, hangars, and most of the original buildings were still intact. At first, the army used the Japanese barracks, but later built Quonset huts to house the units stationed at the camp. When I first arrived, all of the companies of the Second and Third Battalions, except L and M Companies, were housed in Quonset huts. Company M occupied Japanese barracks buildings at the north end of the camp, and L Company lived in an old monastery on a hill overlooking Kunsan. Company L moved from Kunsan to Camp Hillenmeyer in early February.

A map of Camp Hillenmeyer, as I drew it in a letter home, is shown on page 92. Regimental headquarters buildings and services were located in the central portion of the camp. Battalion headquarters were located along the west side of the camp. Each battalion had its own area, with the Quonset huts of each of its companies grouped together as shown on the map. The Japanese air strip ran north and south through the middle of the camp, and three former Japanese hangars were located at the north end of the air strip.

Each platoon had its own Quonset hut and its own sergeant. Each hut had two rooms, a larger one in front that housed about 30 soldiers and a smaller back room that served as living quarters for the platoon sergeant and other noncommissioned officers.

In early March, there was a fire in the central portion of the camp in the regimental headquarters area. In a letter to my parents, dated March 12, I mentioned the fire:

> We had a fire in the camp the other nite about 3 AM. The regimental headquarters burned to the ground. It was a Quonset hut about 50 ft. long.

Not a thing was saved out of the building except the guy that was in it. All records and the message center were totally destroyed.

The population of Camp Hillenmeyer was relatively small when I arrived in January 1947, perhaps 700-800 men. Excluding officers and the personnel essential to serve the very basic needs of the camp, there were only just enough men available for the required guard duty in camp and in Kunsan. Many of the men in camp were due for rotation and looking eagerly toward it.

I was among the first replacements to arrive at the camp since the previous summer. Needless to say, we were welcomed with obvious pleasure. For the next few weeks to months after I arrived, there was a continual influx of men until the population peaked at about 1600-1700. Housing became tight, a dismal situation in view of the extremely cold winter temperatures. In late January, I wrote:

> We got three new guys in this hut the other night. The hut is full now. There's a rumor that we're getting more men and that they are going to live in tents. Poor guys.

The influx continued:

> About ten more new guys came in the other night. About 10 other guys are living in the day room as all the barracks are filled up. A couple of tents are being put up out in back right now so I guess more guys will be coming in.

Tents were put up in a very orderly arrangement throughout the west section of the camp behind the Quonset huts
that housed the companies of the 2nd and 3rd Battalions. I
do not recall how many there were, but behind my Quonset hut alone there were five or six, each holding about 20
men. The tents remained until later in the year, when the
camp population dropped significantly as the result of soldiers being discharged and units being moved to other parts
of South Korea.

Facilities that served the whole camp, such as the Red Cross
Service Club and Post Exchange, were located in the regimental headquarters area. The major attraction of the Red
Cross Service Club was the coffee and donuts they served,
the latter of which were in ample supply when I first arrived at Camp Hillenmeyer. On January 19, I wrote:

> Right now I am in the Red Cross Service Club. It's
> a small place with some tables and chairs scattered
> around. They serve coffee and donuts every few
> hours here, so everybody hangs around here when
> there is nothing to do.

Within two months, as the camp population exploded and
mess hall portions decreased proportionately, donuts became rationed:

> Over here where it is needed, the Red Cross has
> nothing but an office and a free donut for each man
> once a week if he stands in line half a day.

> I'll describe the Red Cross Club as it is, with no ex-
> aggeration. It is a tin building with a wooden floor,

and tables and chairs strategically placed around the room. They play records over a lousy loudspeaker all the time. It sounds more like noise than music. It has a counter at one end with a coffee urn on it. You can have all the coffee you want, providing you bring your own cup.

Despite the fact that I could not get my fill of donuts, I was very grateful to the Red Cross for the free writing paper I made generous use of for my letters home.

The Post Exchange in Camp Hillenmeyer was different from any I had known in the United States, and, like the Red Cross club, was very limited in the service and goods it was able to provide. It was a small place in the regimental headquarters area. As I recall, everything in the PX was rationed. We received weekly ration cards for the few items it carried. Ration-card day was quite an event:

Just about everybody has gone to the PX. tonight as this week's ration cards came due today at 6 PM. There is only one PX in the camp, and the line over there tonite is about a block long. I can't see standing in it when the weather is as cold as it is tonite.

We sure don't get many supplies over here. The ration per week is 3 candy bars, 1 bar of soap, 1 carton of cigarettes, 2 cans of shoestring potatoes, and a can of peanuts. Our weekly ration at the PX comes to about $2.

We could not use U.S. money in the PX. Sometime after leaving Camp Stoneman, our U.S. money must have been exchanged for money issued by the army; however, my first recollection of using invasion money was at the PX in Camp Hillenmeyer. Invasion money reminded me of the paper money used in Monopoly games.

Company mess halls, housed in Quonset huts, were located adjacent to their respective row of company huts. Each company mess hall had its own cook and mess sergeant. When I first arrived at camp, a separate area of our mess hall was screened off for commissioned officers. Privates, called dog robbers, went to the chow line to pick up food for the officers and serve it to them on china plates.

After I was in camp about a month, the officers' club in the regimental headquarters area was finished. That was the last I recall seeing our commissioned officers on a daily basis.

We used our own utensils in the mess hall:

> We stand in the chow line about 5 minutes for break-
> fast after we rinse our mess gear. The water that
> clings to it in small drops freezes solid in that short
> time.

> I guess I had better explain about rinsing our mess
> gear. The silverware, trays and cups are not part of
> the mess hall equipment. Those things are issued
> to us just like clothes. When we come out of the
> mess hall we wash them in 3 garbage cans, one filled
> with hot, soapy water, one disinfectant, and one
> rinse water. We also rinse our stuff before we eat.
> That's the time when the water on them freezes.

There was not enough potable water or soap to waste on the cleaning of pots and cooking utensils. Instead, a truckload of sand from the beach was dumped in back of each mess hall to serve the purpose. The fellows on KP would take all the pots and pans out to the sand pile after a meal was over and scrub them clean with sand.

By March, the dramatic increase in camp population, unaccompanied by an increase in available supplies and equipment, resulted in a scarcity of eating utensils. The time came when we had to share our spoons and forks. No one had both a spoon and a fork, and I did not know anyone who had a knife. As we came out of the mess hall, instead of going over to the three garbage cans to wash our mess gear, we would simply wipe our fork or spoon on our pants leg and hand it to another GI waiting in line. I do not recall washing those I received from other fellows before using them myself. Such things were not that important to me in those days.

There was a small lake-like reservoir, surrounded by a cyclone fence, located among rice paddies near Blacktop Mountain. The reservoir, polluted by water from the rice paddies, was piped into makeshift washrooms, one of which was located behind each company area. The washrooms were shack-like buildings with slab floors, piping from the reservoir, and temperamental boilers to heat the water. On one side of each washroom was a long trough with some primitive faucets and on the other side a shower head or two.

The boilers in the washrooms were constantly breaking down, so warm or hot water was a rarity. In the winter, even cold running water was nonexistent because the pipes froze solid.

In retrospect, the washrooms may not have been intended for use during the winter. American troops had only arrived in Korea during the previous winter, and the water system may have been hastily built to serve immediate needs during the summer of 1946, without consideration for the severe Korean winters. Regardless of the reason, we did not have usable washing facilities during the first half of 1947.

From the time I arrived until about six months later, in June of the same year, the only potable water available came from small tank trailers parked in each company area. The tanks were filled somewhere in a place called the water point, where a small water purification system must have been located.

We were each responsible for keeping our own canteen filled, as necessary, from the water tank trailer. Water from canteens was our sole source of water for drinking and brushing teeth. From time to time during winter months, water for a sponge bath would be obtained by packing a steel helmet with snow and heating the helmet on one of the two stoves in the Quonset hut. When snow was not available, we used water from our canteens. A helmet was made usable as a wash basin by bashing it with a big rock to flatten the top of the helmet so it would stand by itself on a flat surface.

When I first arrived in camp, we could send our clothing to Korean laundresses for washing. However, for some reason unknown to me, this service was ended within a few weeks after I arrived. From that period and until the pipes were repaired in the washrooms, sometime in midyear, our helmets served as our only means for bathing and clothes washing. Because there often was no fuel for the stoves, we frequently had no means to melt snow or heat canteen water. This made bathing and clothes washing next to impossible.

In addition to having laundry service available when I first arrived in camp, for a brief period of time there was a dry cleaning detachment located near one of the old Japanese airplane hangars. The dry cleaning equipment consisted of portable units mounted on truck trailers housed in an area enclosed by a wire fence. All of the soldiers in the dry cleaning unit were black. I do not know where they lived, but their quarters must have been near where they worked. We never saw any black soldiers in camp. It did not occur to me at the time that the army was segregated and that black soldiers were given noncombat roles. The dry cleaning unit disappeared shortly after I arrived. I do not know what happened to it, but I do know it was never replaced.

The difficulties imposed by inadequate washing and cleaning facilities produced a really disreputable-looking group of men. By springtime, we and our clothes were really filthy. As I looked at myself and everyone else around me, I was reminded of the GI's who manned the LSM's that carried us to shore from the Eufaula Victory.

In addition to mess halls and washrooms, each company had its own latrine. The latrines in Camp Hillenmeyer were a lot more fancy than those at Yongdungp'o. At Camp Hillenmeyer they were housed in buildings with slab floors and metal sides and roofs. Along one side of the building were trough urinals. On the wall over the urinal of our company latrine was the elegant sign, "Do Not Piss on Floor or Throw Butts." Since almost all of the men in camp smoked cigarettes, the word butt needed no explanation as it might today.

In the center of each room were eight open-topped 50-gallon drums grouped together in two back-to-back rows of four each. The drums were covered with plywood that had holes chopped out in the appropriate place over each drum. The rough cuts made splinters a not uncommon occurrence. Steps in front of each drum helped the user climb up to the seats. Once a week, a Korean honey wagon, pulled by an ox or scruffy-looking horse, came to clean out the drums. The excrement was used by Korean farmers for fertilizer, the supply of which Camp Hillenmeyer contributed generously.

I do not recall ever seeing a roll of toilet tissue the whole time I was in Korea; however, some must have been available in the latrines at some points in time. I surmise this because a few months before the end of my enlistment, for lack of writing paper, I wrote a letter home on several feet of very thin, hard-finish, unbleached paper about the width of toilet paper. What I do remember is that paperback books and other reading materials, including old issues of the army newspaper *Stars and Stripes* were all we had to serve the purpose. The paperback books were particularly useful because they were printed for the military on very thin paper so they would be light for servicemen to carry.

The most popular recreational facility in camp was located in the hangar area of the camp. One of the Japanese hangars had been converted to a beer hall, known as the Snake Ranch or the IP. All that was sold was coke and beer. As I recall, the brand of beer sold was Prince Rupert and, of course, the coke was Coca Cola. During the winter, the weather was so cold there was no need for refrigeration to cool the drinks.

The beer hall was operated as a nonprofit organization, but it always made so much money that one night a week all beer was free. I did not drink at that time of my life, so I never took advantage of free beer night. In fact, I seldom went to the place because of the smelly lake of urine in front of the building. It was created by the hundreds of GI's who used the area because there was no latrine near the beer hall.

Many of us who did not drink resented the beer hall at times because there was always beer available even when our food portions were meager. In fact, I remember one time when we were having real food shortages, a landing craft with a full load of beer landed somewhere near the camp, perhaps Kunsan harbor. That really angered us. The army could supply us with beer, but not food. It occurred to me recently that I might have fared better if I had been a beer drinker in those days. I would at least have had an ample supply of calories and B vitamins.

There was a movie theater in an old wooden Japanese building. I mentioned the theater numerous times in my letters home:

I went to the movies the other night and saw Bob Hope in 'Monsieur Bocair.' It was really funny. I laughed and laughed. The only trouble is that they had to change reels about 3 times during the picture. Every time it got really good the reel would run out and we'd have to wait about five minutes before the picture started again.

Did I ever describe our theater to you? I will now just in case I didn't before. The name of it is the Shimbu Theater. It is an old Japanese barrack with the windows boarded up. The screen is about 7' x 7'. We sit on benches. That's all there is to it. I've only gone 3 times since I've been here.

I went to the show again last nite and saw 'Home Sweet Homicide.' The only trouble was the ending of the picture wasn't there. It got right up to the climax, the point where the cops are coming and the screen goes blank. You should have heard the moaning the guys did. They finally quieted down and left. That happens with about every picture.

We also had a newsreel. It was about V-J Day. I wouldn't say that was old or anything.

A service company detachment occupied a vacant hangar by the air strip. Their trucks and equipment were kept in a fenced area by the hangar. The service company was the transportation system for Camp Hillenmeyer. They drove cargo and trucked in our food, clothing, and other supplies.

They also transported troops as needed. It must have been trucks from the service company that brought us from the railroad station in Iri to Camp Hillenmeyer.

Contrary to my first impression during the drive from Iri, the drivers from the service company were really pretty nice fellows when you got to know them. Because of my interest in engines, I talked to some of the drivers about why the trucks were so terribly noisy. They told me that they were not able to maintain the trucks properly because there was a severe shortage of replacement parts. As a result, the trucks had no mufflers.

The drivers showed me how they had solved the problem caused by a lack of exhaust system parts. When an original exhaust pipe and muffler system failed, the mechanics welded a homemade fitting to a long piece of 2-inch diameter iron water pipe so that the water pipe could be bolted to the exhaust manifold. The pipe ran from the manifold down under the truck and terminated at the back. This carried the exhaust and the noise out back and away from the cab. I was really impressed with their ingenuity in converting an unusable machine into a usable one by making do with whatever materials they had at hand.

I referred to the sorry state of the motor pool in a letter home:

> You say there isn't much news about Korea. One reason is that there is not much over here to write about that would accredit anybody. I think the army is ashamed to release the truth about this

place. Take our motor pool for instance. It has 40
vehicles assigned to it and only 7 are running and
they are shot. That's the way everything is.

Interestingly, the number of operating vehicles was soon
to decrease to only six. The casualty was a reliable six-by-
six with a rarely-seen steel cab and windows that closed, a
very nice feature in a frigid place like Korea — our other
vehicles had canvas tops and no doors at all. We knew that
our reliable truck had been borrowed (stolen) from another
army unit and brought from the Philippines to Korea in
October 1945 by the troops of 63rd Infantry. Apparently
more than one truck was liberated and brought to Korea at
that time (Munschauer, page 158).

Unfortunately, our reliable truck was not long for this
world. One day, there was an inspection by some supply
officer. He found that the serial number on the truck did
not appear on the official inventory of the 63rd Infantry.
The army, in a display of studied incompetence, solved the
problem by ordering some men from Service Company to
push the truck off a nearby bluff into the Yellow Sea. What
a waste! The truck was badly needed, and it was obviously owned by the army. Most important, its destruction
showed gross disrespect for the American people who had
paid for the truck with their hard earned money.

Camp Hillenmeyer underwent considerable improvement
and expansion during the latter half of 1947. During that
period, in my final assignment, I participated in that effort.

CHAPTER NINE

THE WIRE PLATOON

I felt very lucky to have landed by an act of fate in the wire platoon of a battalion headquarters company. I was especially encouraged the first night in camp after talking with the fellows who had been there a while about the work they were doing. I felt I would learn a lot from these men.

One of the duties of the wire platoon was to provide telephone service for the 3rd Battalion. This involved operating the battalion switchboard, known as "Guard Blue," 24 hours a day and maintaining the wires of the communications system. The switchboard was connected to the orderly rooms of all of the companies in the 3rd Battalion, including M Company in the Japanese barracks and L Company in the monastery in Kunsan. Also connected to our switchboard were regimental headquarters and several other buildings in the camp.

The morning after I arrived I met our platoon sergeant, a man by the name of Lipscomb. I questioned him further about the work of the platoon and asked him if there were any special materials I should study. His only advice was to hang around with the fellows who ran the headquarters switchboard located in a nearby Quonset hut.

Sergeant Lipscomb was very kind to me, but it was obvious he was a rather depressed man. He had been in Korea for a long time, probably from the time Camp Hillenmeyer was established, and was looking forward to being rotated. I thought it interesting that he wanted to be rotated rather than discharged, but he was a professional soldier and perhaps was looking forward to a better duty station. Sergeant Lipscomb said he was very tired of pulling almost constant guard duty, a duty unusual for sergeants. However, the camp was so shorthanded that everyone had to take turns guarding the facilities of the camp even to the neglect of their regular duties. The camp was surrounded by a population that was not hostile but very hungry, so it took a lot of guards to protect the camp against stealing.

During the first few days at Camp Hillenmeyer, I had to pinch myself often to make sure I was not dreaming. I could not believe that life at Camp Hillenmeyer, an army camp half way around the world in a country so different from what I had ever known, was so much more civilized than any other place I had been in the army. The Quonset huts we lived in were not crowded. Reveille was at the respectable hour of 6:45 AM, and we were wakened by a real live bugler. In Korea, human buglers replaced the loudspeaker systems we had known in the States.

Even more gratifying to me than being able to sleep a little later in the morning was the fact that the army employed

Korean civilians to do many of the unpleasant jobs that GI's did in the States. Each Quonset hut had a Korean houseboy who swept the hut, hung up our clothes, and in general kept the hut neat and clean. Koreans were also employed to work in the mess halls, performing the KP duties that were the bane of enlisted men in the States. I could not believe that I would have no more KP.

The employment of Korean service people was discontinued in early March, just two months after I arrived in camp. We had no idea why, but the rumor around camp was that they were terminated because of severe food shortages; the army no longer had sufficient supplies to feed both the Korean workers and the soldiers.

Sometime later I learned that the houseboys and mess hall workers also made arrangements for the services of young Korean women. The enlisted men I lived with at that time were all relatively unsophisticated kids like me and, as such, were not particularly convinced that this added amenity was in our best interest. Thus, we had little firsthand knowledge of the logistics involved. However, a small hut three doors away held about a dozen enlisted who men opted for such pleasures, much to their regret; soon after, six of them were diagnosed with gonorrhea.

Prostitutes were not a prominent feature at Camp Hillenmeyer, but their presence was never very far away. The perimeter of the camp was too long to be fenced or guarded because of the large size of the airfield. Thus, with a little care, anyone, including prostitutes, could walk in and out of camp during nighttime hours.

Our first several weeks in Camp Hillenmeyer were a continuation of basic training. Those of us who arrived in camp on the same day were grouped together for training. We learned more about our rifles, how to use them and care for them. However, we never once had target practice. I took apart and cleaned my rifle innumerable times, but I never fired it at all the whole time I was in South Korea.

We not only cleaned our rifles over and over again during the first few weeks, but we also marched and marched in what seemed like an endless journey to nowhere. One morning a week, with backpacks and rifles, we hiked for about six to eight miles. The hikes took us over all the same places inside and outside of the camp:

> We have a 6-mile hike every Wednesday morning with light pack and rifle. Last week we walked along the beach then inland thru a few native villages. It took 2 hours and was more of a sight-seeing tour than anything.

Although we walked in formation, many of the hikes were really interesting and did not seem like training exercises. We hiked along the beach, through rice paddies, up and down mountains, and through villages.

In addition to military training, we performed various details around the camp and did a lot of guard duty. Guard duty was assigned by a notice on the company bulletin board. A notice listed about 75 names, with each name assigned a post number and a relief. The notice also included general instructions specifying uniform and when and where to report. Guard duty was divided into three reliefs (shifts), with the first starting at 6:00 PM, the second at 8:00 PM, and the third at 10:00 PM. Each relief was two hours on duty and four hours off duty for 24 hours.

We reported for guard duty at a designated place, usually in a nearby open field, one hour before the start of our 24-hour assignment. There we waited for the Officer of the Day, who took roll call and conducted inspection. Inspections were fairly casual, of necessity. We did not have the wherewithall for a spit and polish presentation. We were dirty because we lacked adequate bathing facilities. And our uniforms were shabby because of the absence of supplies of new clothing.

After inspection, we were marched to a guard house, usually a cold, empty building, where we had to stay, shivering, during our off duty hours. We were each issued a clip of ammunition that we had to return at the end of our assignment. Any missing bullets had to be accounted for. As time approached for a relief to begin, a truck would arrive to take us to our assigned posts.

My first guard duty occurred on my tenth day in camp, January 20. Five days later, I wrote:

> January 20th is the Korean New Year. All these people become a year older on that day so they have a big celebration that lasts a week. All of the Koreans that work on the post did not come to work until today.

> I pulled guard duty the nite of the 20th and the day of the 21st — of all times. That's my luck. All the

guards were doubled that nite as trouble was expected, but nothing happened. The post I had was
about 2 miles from camp. There were 2 of us on it
and 2 across the road. That really was a dark nite.
We didn't see the 2 across the road until daylite.
We could hear the Koreans yelling and making a
lot of noise all around until about midnite. Things
quieted down then.

My first guard duty was at what I later found out to be an
ammunition dump. The bulletin board had me on third
relief and gave me post number 16, in this case a number I
will never forget. When the time came for third relief, I got
into the back of a truck along with about ten other guards.
We were told to jump out when our post number was called.
When my number was called, another fellow jumped out
with me. Without so much as a word, the two guards that
we had relieved hopped in the truck, and the truck sped
away into the darkness. The fellow who jumped off the
truck with me and I looked at one another and introduced
ourselves. We had never met before.

The night was bitterly cold with several inches of snow on
the ground. It was 10 o'clock at night and pitch dark, so
dark that we could see no further than a few feet. There
was a barbwire fence along the road and a gate leading
into what we had heard might be an ammunition dump.
Neither one of us had ever set foot in the place before.

With only five weeks of basic training in the States, and no
orientation or training for guard duty in Korea, we had
absolutely no idea of how to respond to problems that might
arise. We were not told what we were supposed to guard

against or even what the facility we were guarding looked like. No one told us what was inside the facility or how we should guard it. Were we supposed to guard the gate? Because anyone could easily slip through the barbwire fence, were we supposed to look for people inside? Most important, we were given no instructions on whether to place the clip of ammunition in our rifles while on guard duty or the conditions under which we should shoot. Old-timers in camp provided our only guidance. Their words of wisdom were, "If you shoot any Koreans, be sure to place some item of military property near the body and say you fired because the person was stealing and refused your re-peated commands to halt."

In the absence of instructions, my fellow guard and I de-cided to walk through the gate to see what was inside. We also decided that, because it was so very dark, we might lose our sense of direction if we went very far inside the gate. If we did, we might not be able to find our way back by midnight when the truck was coming to drop off our replacements and bring us back to the guard house.

Being curious yet cautious, we decided we would walk along the inside of the barbwire fence. One of us would go in one direction along the fence and the other in the oppo-site direction until we met. We assumed that the fence sur-rounded the entire facility. However, we decided if we did not meet in about a half hour, we would retrace our steps and follow the fence back to the gate. Fortunately, the fence did surround the facility.

After fumbling along the fence in the darkness, my fellow guard and I met on a slight hill about ten minutes away from the entry gate. At this point, we reversed course and made our way back to the gate, where we would meet again. As we walked back and forth along the fence, we could hear a low level commotion in the distance. We knew there were a lot of poor and hungry people around who would slip into camp at night and take whatever they could carry away. We also knew that we were out of earshot of anyone who could come help us if we got into trouble.

Later the next morning, during our 10:00 AM to noon shift, we saw that the fence was, in fact, around an ammunition dump. The fence surrounded an area of about 20 acres of low, rolling hills sparsely covered by stunted pine trees. Inside were two or three ammunition bunkers, open at each end, in which artillery shells were stacked.

I was a terrified, inexperienced 19-year old kid that first night on guard duty. I was alone and afraid in an unknown and alien territory, inhabited by hungry, desperate people with whom I could not communicate. With time, I gained experience at guard duty, but I never lost the fear. It always accompanied me on guard duty at night.

Fortunately, we were safer than we knew at Camp Hillenmeyer. I never heard of a soldier being harmed, or even accosted, while on guard duty at the camp. However, other areas of South Korea were not as safe. While I was at Camp Hillenmeyer, two soldiers from the 63rd Infantry were killed by intruders while on guard duty at a supply base called Ascom City, near Inch'on.

My lack of live training with the M-1 rifle issued to me when I arrived at camp contributed to my worry about guard duty. I had never fired the rifle, and did not even know if it would fire. Some of the older enlisted men told us that many of the M-1 rifles had faulty firing pins and probably were not capable of being fired. To make matters worse, we were issued only one clip, eight bullets, when we went on guard duty. Eight bullets would have been of little value if we ever had any real trouble. Thus, I always carried my bayonet whenever I went on guard duty. Later, when stealing became more prevalent, guards were issued 12-gauge repeater shot guns and encouraged to shoot. I was glad I was no longer doing guard duty then.

During off duty hours there was little to do. I spent a lot of time with the fellows who ran the switchboard, trying to learn all I could about its operation. The time I spent with them paid off. Before the end of my training, I wrote:

> I'm writing this letter from the radio shack, which is next door to my hut. It's a lot lighter and quieter here.

> I learned how to operate the switchboard this morning. It's a small one for the 3rd Bn with only 18 phones on it. I might have to operate it sometime. I don't know yet.

> There is a big short wave radio in here so we listen to stations all over the world. We heard the Hit Parade this morning from New York. We also get Australia, Chonju and Seoul, Korea, and Hawaii. It is really nice to hear stuff straight from the states. I'm listening to the latest news from Los Angeles right now.

Two days later, I was a real happy fellow:

> I finally got a regular job. I am through with drill-
> ing — I hope. I'm now a switchboard operator. I
> work five hours a day and am off every 4th day. I
> like it because I'm inside out of the weather.
>
> We guys on the board work sort of a rotating shift.
> One day 7 AM to noon; next day noon to 5 PM;
> next day 5 PM to 9 PM and sleep all nite in the ra-
> dio shack just in case they need it at night, which
> they never do. I sleep just as good in there as in the
> barracks. Next day off.
>
> The switchboard is located in the Radio Shack so it
> doesn't get monotonous. There are always some
> guys in there sending messages on the radio. When
> I am off I can horse around in there. There are all
> kinds of Japanese radios, batteries, and junk around.
> I also keep pretty well posted as the radio in there
> will pick up almost any part of the world.

I had a big surprise one day while operating the switchboard. I was talking to the switchboard operator in Kunsan
on some official business when the fellow on the other end
said, "Is that you, Ottoboni?" It was my friend Mette, whom
I had not seen since we left the Eufaula Victory. If he had
not recognized my voice, I would not have known that he
was in Kunsan.

During my free time I did a lot of letter writing, walking
on the beach, and exploring the camp. During one of my

explorations of the regimental headquarters area I found the Information and Education (I&E) Detachment. There I learned about the United States Armed Forces Institute (USAFI). I decided it would be a good use of my spare time to take some courses, but no application blanks were available. Finally, when applications did come to I&E, I filled one out and sent in my two-dollar application fee for a calculus course. I did eventually receive a calculus book, but nothing else ever arrived.

Mail service was very erratic the whole time I was in Korea. By the end of my first month at Camp Hillenmeyer, I still had not received any mail:

> The mail system around here is pretty poor. Hardly anybody gets mail. The guys that have been here for 2 or 3 months get mail very seldom. I haven't received any yet, but I'm still hoping.

When letters finally arrived, they came in bunches. The same was true with packages, except they took longer en route. I knew from letters that my mother had sent a number of packages, but none had arrived by mid-March:

> I haven't received any packages yet, but don't worry about them. I'm sure they'll get here eventually. The guys are still getting Christmas packages.

Two weeks later I received three packages in one day. Whenever any of us received a package, we all shared our booty. Thus, the arrival of goodies from home was a noisy and welcome occasion for the whole hut:

When I get packages I really get them. Boy, what a surprise! Everybody watched me open them with their tongues hanging out. That happens when anybody gets a package. You have a big 'Thank you' from the Commo hut for your very delicious cookies. Boy that stuff really hit the spot as the PX has been closed for a week. We really enjoyed Bob's cookies. They were the best.

I'll tell you what was in the packages so you'll know which ones got here. One had canned peaches, olives, deviled meat, crackers, chap stick (that's handy), hard candy and cookies. I ate the whole can of peaches by myself all at once. Were they good. We ate the crackers and olives in the radio shack. We had a swell time. Everyone shares their packages over here.

The next package had some walnuts and a box of McFarlands Candy. I saved the candy for myself and gave away the nuts. We ate the big can of cookies out of the next box. They were also very good. I still have the other cookies, dried apricots and magazines and papers. Thanks again for everything.

We spent off duty hours in the evenings chatting with one another and sometimes singing old songs. There was not much else we could do because we seldom had light. The problems with electricity were due in large part to the fact that the power came from North Korea. There were a few diesel generators at the mess halls and headquarters buildings, but electricity for the living quarters was generated somewhere north of the 38th parallel. At times, the lack of lighting was depressing:

> This electric power we use here comes from the Russian Zone of Korea and it's pretty lousy. These barracks are so dark that we can't read at nite. That's what makes the place so monotonous. If I could only lay down and read for a couple of hours at nite. As it is now I come in and talk for a while and go to bed.

At other times we were resourceful:

> The lights are out again tonite, but that doesn't stop us from writing or from having light. We improvise. Right now we are using a can of dubbing with a piece of rope for a wick. It's a little smoky, but it gives off more light than a candle.

We could be even more resourceful in the radio shack because there was so much more to work with:

> The lights just went out again but that didn't bother us. We rigged up a light with some batteries and things are as bright as ever.

> This radio shack is really loaded with batteries of all kinds. Since the lights have been going out about every nite, the boys have been rigging up lights of all types. I built a flashlight last night that is pretty good. I'll draw you a plan of it. What do you think? [of enclosed diagram] Anyway I had a good time making it.

About six weeks after arrival at Camp Hillenmeyer, I was
on my way to being a full-fledged lineman:

> They're starting to train us guys in the wire section
> in laying field telephones and stuff. That training
> is from 8 AM to noon when I am not on the switch-
> board. I'm sure glad I got this job. From now on I
> won't be getting anymore guard duty. That suits
> me fine.

Actually, guard duty and KP did not end when I became a
lineman, but they occurred much less often. Despite the
occasional guard duty and KP, I enjoyed my assignment
and found it interesting:

> At 8 AM the motor pool guys leave and the wire
> section, which includes me and about 3 other guys,
> goes over to the regimental switchboard shack. We
> go over there every morning to help the regimen-
> tal wire section keep up their lines.

> About 10:30 this morning we went over to the mo-
> tor pool office and fixed a few wires. Somebody
> wired the place that didn't know what he was do-
> ing. It's a wonder the place hasn't burned down.
> All the office is is a shack with no ceiling so the job
> was a cinch. We finished at noon.

> This afternoon we went over to the Colonel's house
> and tried to fix his phone, but we didn't have a jeep
> to ride along the wire to check it, so we quit for the
> day. We'll fix it tomorrow when there is more time.
> Anyway we had only 3 men. There'll be more of

us tomorrow to stand around with intelligent looks
on our faces. Give us time — we'll fix it.

In addition to routine maintenance, there were always
emergencies that made extra work for the wire platoon.
The fire that destroyed the regimental headquarters Quonset hut was a case in point:

> That caused a lot of work for us as 9 phones burned
> in the building and we had to install new ones in
> other buildings to take the place of the burnt ones.

> There's nothing to putting up one of these army
> phones. All you do is hook up two wires to the 2
> lugs on the phone and start unrolling wire to where
> you're going.

> We had to fix another line yesterday afternoon.
> Somebody cut the line to the officers quarters. We
> walked along with a test phone and in no time
> found where the wire was cut. We spliced it to-
> gether and it's as good as new now.

The field telephones were the hand-cranked variety housed
in a stiff, rectangular leather case about the size of a
woman's handbag. The leather case held the telephone
hand piece and a large dry cell battery. A vigorous turning
of the crank on the side of the case caused another directly-
connected telephone to ring.

I was very interested in all of the equipment in the wire
platoon. I wrote home about one that was completely new
to me:

I was a radio operator 'per force' a couple of days ago. We had an alert and expected that some Koreans would cut the telephone line between here and Kunsan so we set up two walkie talkies in Kunsan, one at the M.P. station and one at L Company which is on a hill overlooking Kunsan. I operated the one at the M.P. station for a day. I shot the bull with the guy that was up at L Company.

Those walkie talkies work darn good. They're just like a telephone. I didn't even have it outside. It worked right inside the building.

The military telephone system at Camp Hillenmeyer was very simple in comparison to today's systems. A telephone line consisted of two braided strands of insulated copper wire. Inside the camp, these lines were mostly laid on the ground beside the roads. Such lines connected our switchboard with field telephones located in the various company orderly rooms and command posts. Between camp and Kunsan, the lines were also laid alongside the road, but inside Kunsan they were hung on existing power poles or trees.

In order to work on the wires in Kunsan, we learned to climb poles and trees using the same steel spur climbers used by utility linemen in the states. Climbing was serious business because a slip caused by lack of attention or a rotten pole could mean a serious fall. We were lucky, no one fell.

Our wire repair expeditions to Kunsan were interesting for me because I was the only greenhorn. Three of us would take a jeep and, along with the wire section's mascot — a small, well-trained dog — drive to the work site. When we stopped to work, the dog would jump on the hood of the jeep and keep the usual crowd of curious Koreans far enough away so they could not steal our gear.

Newly arrived from the States, and still a teenager, I was wide-eyed at how my coworkers entertained themselves and their Korean spectators when working on telephone wires. One day, while high on a pole in a busy part of Kunsan, the usual small crowd had gathered below to watch. My friend on the pole yelled down to me. "Watch this," he said, and then stood on one of the crossbars and proceeded to urinate on the crowd below. I could not believe what I saw!

Strangely, nobody got mad. They just giggled and backed away and kept staring up at my friend. On the drive back to camp I could not hold back my questions — and my amazement. I was told that Koreans enjoyed this horseplay because they had heard that American male organs were of extraordinary size, and they were anxious to see this for themselves.

CHAPTER TEN

THE FIRST WINTER: HUNGER AND COLD

Every one of us who arrived at Camp Hillenmeyer on that bleak night in early January soon learned what it was like to be hungry, cold, and dirty.

I was one of the few lucky ones whose duffel bag was not bounced out into the darkness and lost forever on the rough 30-mile trip from the railroad station in Iri to the 63rd Infantry at Camp Hillenmeyer. Many of the men lost everything, and the army had essentially no replacement shoes, socks, or other clothing. The unfortunate ones who lost their bags were resupplied inadequately, but as well as they could be under the circumstances, from shoes and clothing taken from soldiers returning to the States.

I found it hard to believe that any United States Army installation could be so ill supplied, particularly at that time when tons of surplus clothing and other gear left over from World War II were being sold as surplus at home.

We new arrivals quickly learned that life at Hillenmeyer would not be pleasant. We were told upon arrival that all of the local water and food in Korea was dangerously polluted. We were instructed not to eat anything except from the mess hall and not to drink any water except that from a water tank mounted on a two-wheel trailer parked outside the mess hall. This water came from an army-operated water point and was hauled daily from Kunsan. We were told to keep our canteens filled from the trailer and to use only this water for drinking and brushing our teeth.

Many things were wrong. There was not enough food. During the winter and spring of 1947, there was rarely a time when I was not uncomfortably hungry. We were always cold and often slept with all our clothes on. There was not enough fuel to heat our Quonset huts, and not enough cold weather clothing, gloves, and shoes to protect us adequately when we were outdoors, particularly at night. As new arrivals filled the camp the problems became worse. In my first letter home, I noted the shortage of food:

> The food here is good. The cooks do a good job. However, we don't get too much of it. It's enough, but I don't get stuffed like I did at Stoneman.

Actually, for the first time in my life, I felt half-starved all the time. Hunger was an almost constant companion, but

I stopped complaining about it in letters home because I did not want to worry my mother. However, I did ask her to send food in almost every letter I wrote:

> Here's a request for a package as I sure could use something besides army chow. Those 3 candy bars we get every week sure go down fast. I eat them all the first nite. Don't send candy bars though unless they're easy to get. Send anything edible. I'll be satisfied with anything.

> When I get back, you won't hear me complain about anything. I'll eat whatever you happen to throw in front of me.

When I arrived in Korea, I weighed 150 pounds; three months later, I weighed 120 pounds. At my normal weight, I had been called skinny. Despite orders to the contrary, I bought food from Korean vendors on my first pass to Kunsan. Although I did not realize it at the time, my experience in Kunsan gave a clue to a small part of the much larger problem responsible for the many shortages of supplies and equipment in camp:

> I went to Kunsan on pass yesterday. I had 1400 yen when I started and I just about spent it all. I bought a carton of Lifesavers for 500 yen. We can't even get candy in the PX and the Koreans have it to sell. That's something I can't see.

> I also bought 20 eggs for 300 yen and 5 cans of corned beef hash. The hash is the same as we get in the mess hall. I think the people who handle the

food sell it to the Koreans. Then the Koreans turn
around and sell it back to us.

I'm not being different or anything when I buy eggs
and stuff. All the guys do. We cook them in the
barracks at nite.

Another food item I remember purchasing from Koreans,
when nothing better was available, was rock candy. For a
while during that first winter, it was a significant source of
food for us. The Koreans seemed to have a never-ending
supply of rock candy, but, because we were hungry and
desperate for food, we did not question its source. The
rock candy came in one gallon cans painted olive drab with
some English letters that I cannot recall stenciled on them.
Many years later I learned of the probable source of the
rock candy from a paper by Edward W. Wagner:

And I well remember the outrage of a young Korean friend when it was made known that a mountain of rock candy somehow left behind on Okinawa
would be brought to Korea as a bonus item in the
U.S. aid and relief program. 'Has your government,' he asked, 'no interest in our minds? We can
survive without sugar, or candy, with only the most
basic daily necessities, but we cannot survive without books.' (Wagner, page 24)

What surplus rock candy was doing in Okinawa, I have
yet to learn.

We were always hungry. In fact, food shortage became so
severe that one morning in early March, a number of huts

in the 3rd Battalion actually staged what might be called a mutiny, although a relatively brief one. On that morning, I woke up to grumblings that we were not going to fall out unless we got more food. Having been in Korea only a short time, I was at a loss to know what was happening. When the whistle blew to fall out, nobody moved. I do not know what happened in the other huts, but a noncommissioned officer came in to our hut to tell us to get off our butts and fall out. Again, no one moved.

Then another noncommissioned officer came in brandishing a pistol. He told us that he would shoot anyone who refused to fall out. At that point, I realized the revolt must have been planned because some fellows in the back of the hut stood up and said they had guns, too, and that they would shoot him if he shot any of us. Nobody moved. I looked around the hut at the other guys. The faces I saw were grim and unyielding. I watched in disbelief, too stunned to be frightened, and thought, "Whoa, what in the world am I in the middle of?"

Despite my fright, I sympathized with the mutineers because I was so hungry and had lost so much weight. My mind raced from one thought to another. I was deeply disturbed and asked myself why I didn't immediately run out of the hut and leave the group. But, severe hunger is so powerful a drive that it can change a person's whole value system. What may happen next week or next month becomes unimportant. The present is all that matters. I suddenly realized that my perception of risk had changed. I was no longer fearful of confrontation. In those very few moments, I learned that continual hunger and cold can change loyalties. I stayed in the hut.

Many years later, I was struck by the words of the late Marguerite Higgins, a war combat correspondent during the Korean War:

> You can't have a working democracy where people are starving. Hunger breeds desperation; desperation breeds violence; violence breeds a police state. (Higgins, page 218)

Ms. Higgins was referring to the Korean people, but the words aptly described the situation in our hut on that desperate morning.

Fortunately, violence was averted in our situation. The noncommissioned officer left and a short time later our company commander came in to see us. He was obviously a much more wise man than the pistol packer. He said he understood our complaint and that he would make every effort to see that we got more food. He talked to us about the camp population pressures and the difficulties they were having getting adequate supplies. He talked to us and he listened to us. He said he would tell the mess sergeant to give us more food for breakfast that morning. We all gave up and went to the mess hall. That ended our mutiny once and for all.

Several years later, when I was attending Stanford University on the GI Bill, I met that same company commander on the steps of the main library. I cannot recall his name. He was still in the military, but assigned to attend Stanford in some sort of a masters degree program. Our meeting was cordial, but brief. After we parted, I wondered why we really didn't talk. After all, we had been fellow soldiers. He was a decent company commander, but we had little in common. He was pursuing a career in the military and I had a different life plan.

I never wrote home about our mutiny. However, my mother, apparently worried about my constant requests for food, wrote to the War Department on March 11, 1947. The three-page response from Major General Edward F. Witsell, dated 28 March, 1947, included the following denial that there was any problem:

> In a report received in this office concerning the conditions in Korea the following facts are set forth: 'All messes draw a 10-day supply of perishable foods, which includes fresh meats, fruits and vegetables... Each mess is required to serve three hot meals a day to all troops... The master menu for troops in Korea authorizes a minimum of 4,000 calories per man per day, which is about 400 calories in excess of that allowed military personnel in the United States...In this connection, the report indicates that practically every soldier has been getting three hot substantial hot meals a day and that all troops, whether in garrison or on patrol duty, receive at least the minimum 4,000 calories per day...'

I am sure that my mother's letter, *per se*, was not responsible for the events that followed. The army was probably swamped with letters from irate parents of young men like myself who were not professional soldiers. Everyone else I knew in camp complained in letters home about lack of food, winter clothing, washing facilities, heat, and so forth. Regardless of the cause, on April 11, 1947, I wrote home:

We've had a 2-star general inspecting the camp
these last few days. Our company was the first one
he inspected and he came without notice so you
can imagine what a mess he found. I don't think
he was too well-impressed with the whole thing.
He bawled out our C.O. and in turn the C.O. is fix-
ing us.

The repercussions from the General's visit lasted for several weeks:

I'm lucky I'm still a Pfc as 26 guys got busted to
Pvts in the last 2 days for minor offenses such as
having dented helmets, having water in canteens
and other slight infractions. It's lucky that I was
thirsty the night before inspection and drank my
canteen dry. Beginner's luck.

The cause of all this busting was Gen. Brown who
came in without notice, found the place a little
messed up and bawled out our C.O. From there on
it was the old army game of passing the buck and
we guys finally got the works. Things are cooling
off now so I guess we'll be back to normal soon.

We felt our punishment unfair because most of us had been
issued helmets that were already dented. Almost all of the
helmets in camp had been deliberately dented so they could
stand alone and serve as wash basins. Also, when we arrived at camp we were told to keep our canteens filled with
purified water from the tank trailer parked near the mess
hall to use for drinking and brushing teeth. However, de-

spite what we considered unfairness, inspections and pun-
ishments continued:

> We had some more inspections of the barracks last
> week by a bunch of big shots. All they do is in-
> spect, they never improve conditions. It seems that
> the 1st Sarge didn't like the way my bed was made
> up. He didn't like Prinzo's, or Walker's, Kelly's
> and a lot of other guys. Anyway, we spent Sat. af-
> ternoon on KP.

Despite it all, we were pleased that at least the food situation improved:

> Take it a little easy on sending packages from now
> on as now we are getting plenty to eat. We now
> can get all the ice cream we want at the service club.
> For 10¢ you get a whole canteen cup full which is
> at least a pint. The guys have really been eating it.
> Every once in a while somebody will bring a whole
> 5 gallon container of it and pass it out in the hut.

> The food here now is as good as can be expected.
> For breakfast this morning I had 5 pancakes, 2
> pieces of toast and butter, 1 hardboiled egg, 2 apples
> and a cup of coffee. That was all I could eat. I could
> have more if I wanted it.

> That was a big improvement from what we used to
> get. A typical breakfast a month ago was 2 fried
> eggs and coffee. No bread or anything. We were
> really hungry then. We used to like KP because it

was the only time you could get full. Things are
different now so don't worry about me being hungry anymore.

Despite occasional feasts, we were sustained for the most
part by packages from home and purchases, primarily eggs,
from the Koreans. After a few weeks the food situation
returned to its former state in both quantity and variety:

The chow is pretty good on the whole. The only
thing we get a lot of is potatoes.

We don't get any fresh milk around here at all, but
we sure get a lot of canned and dried milk. I'm
getting used to it now and it tastes as good as fresh
milk.

In retrospect, I believe that the bouts of illness that frequently landed me in the hospital were nutritionally based.
During the first winter (1946-47), the food provided us was
so limited that, as mentioned earlier, my weight had
dropped from 150 to 120 pounds in three months. In addition, our very small meals never included any fresh fruits,
or green vegetables, and seldom included fresh meat, despite General Witsell's assurances to my mother.

I am convinced that the underlying reason for the severe
colds, sore throats, intractable skin problems, and trench
mouth (scurvy?) I suffered were the direct result of the prolonged period in which we were fed an inadequate diet. I
regained my weight after I returned to civilian life, but skin
and gum problems remained with me for many years, despite medical attention from Veterans Administration and

private physicians and dentists. These problems slowly disappeared after I began heavily supplementing my diet with essential nutrients such as vitamin C.

Despite illnesses that resulted in frequent and futile trips to the camp hospital, I did feel that I was getting good medical care:

> I'm not saying they don't take care of you. Every slight ailment a person might have is given plenty of attention. The only trouble is they don't send you any farther than Korea. They take care of you right here unless you get something that there is no cure for. I'm not complaining. I feel fine now and every time I have been sick I have been well cared for.

I was not alone in having frequent minor medical problems. Many of us in camp noted that any small cuts or scratches became very red around the edges and took much longer than normal to heal.

Although I had not said so directly in my letters home, my mother had a strong suspicion that all was not well with my living conditions. She was particularly worried about my frequent hospitalizations, and suggested that I transfer to another unit. I responded in a letter on June 28:

> You suggested that I try to get transferred to a better climate. We are forgotten men. Nobody gets transfers no matter what happens. I know one guy that has sinus so bad that he can't sleep nights. The doctors admit he should leave but he is still here.

Actually, I found one transfer that was possible. It was to the 11th Airborne Division that, at that time, was located in Hokaido, Japan. However, to qualify for the transfer, one had to enlist for another three years and, of course, be willing to jump out of airplanes!

In addition to lack of food and clothing, lack of heating fuel was a serious problem in the bitterly cold winter months. When I first arrived at Camp Hillenmeyer, coal was the fuel used for heating. In our hut there was a small pot bellied stove and a stove made from a 50-gallon oil drum. On one of my first nights in camp we had to do first aid on the potbelly:

> It was a little smoky in the hut tonight. We lit a fire in one of the coal stoves a little while ago and it started smoking.
>
> The hut got so smoky that you could hardly see the other end. We figured that the smoke pipe was stopped up so a couple of us went up on the roof and ran a stick thru it. That stopped the smoking and things are back to normal.

A few days later our coal supplies, which came from North Korea, were exhausted. Apparently it was decided that supplies of diesel oil would be more reliable, so some of the stoves in the camp were converted to oil burners. Our pot bellied stove did not appreciate the change:

> Things are blacker than ever now that we converted over to oil. The stove keeps getting plugged up about every hour and we have to take it apart and

clean it out. In the process a lot of smoke and soot gets out into the hut. Oh well, it's like they say over here, 'things are rough overseas.'

In actual fact, supplies of diesel fuel were no more reliable than coal. The oil came in 50-gallon drums from the States to Inch'on and from there by train to Kunsan. The barrels did not always reach Kunsan. They were either sold or stolen along with other supplies and equipment, somewhere between Inch'on and Kunsan. One very common method of stealing fuel was to partially empty the drums and replace the missing diesel fuel or gasoline with water. Thus, the weight of the individual drums did not change significantly, and the theft would not be discovered until the drums were opened at their final destination. Watered drums caused a great deal of trouble for everybody, but particularly for those trying to keep our vehicles running.

Because of the problems with diesel fuel, we continued to burn coal when it was available. When we had neither diesel nor coal, we burned whatever we could find:

> The camp is out fuel for heating purposes. We haven't had any diesel for a week and we're also out of coal. All there is to burn is wood and that is getting scarce. We have burned everything that isn't nailed down and we're starting on stuff that is nailed down. If we don't get some coal pretty soon there isn't going to be a camp left.

To cope with the shortage of coal and fuel oil, details of soldiers were sent out to collect and chop into stove-size pieces any scrap wood that could be found in the camp.

As a result of this effort, a very large pile of firewood was accumulated in an open area behind our row of Quonset huts for us to use as fuel.

Shortly after the wood became available for use as fuel, two men from K Company were badly injured by an explosion while gathering wood from the pile. An immediate military investigation showed that the wood pile had been secretly booby-trapped by a colonel, newly arrived from Japan, who was hoping to catch Koreans who were stealing wood from the pile

We were never told why the soldiers who used the wood pile were not warned of this special hazard. Talk in the hut, based on rumor, was that this colonel had been transferred from a U.S. military unit in Japan as punishment for poor performance. At the time, these rumors seemed unbelievable to me. Why would incompetent officers be sent to supervise us? Many years later, I learned that the rumors had a basis in fact. General Hodge, while Commander of the occupation forces in Korea, was very concerned about the quality of the officers and men assigned to him:

> When officers were assigned to the Far Eastern Command, Tokyo skimmed off the cream of the personnel and left the rest for Hodge...

> ...He [Hodge] was displeased at the personnel coming his way, particularly the officers...And MacArthur's headquarters simply added to his woes by treating assignment to Korea as punishment. (One young soldier was offered his choice of court-martial or Korea.) (Smith, pp.18-35)

After the pile of scrap wood was burned, we broke up unused canvas cots for fuel. When all empty cots were consumed, we turned to those newly unoccupied. Shortly after someone was transferred out, his cot disappeared. When there were no more cots, we turned to unused structures.

One of the structures that disappeared was an old wooden building that had been abandoned partially finished, perhaps by the Japanese. It was a wood frame structure approximately 20' x 40' consisting of a floor, walls, and roof. It had been located in a field that was scheduled to become a parade ground. In late January, about 100 of us were detailed to physically lift and move the building about 50 yards away to the edge of the field.

Parenthetically, it was interesting to see what 100 people can lift. First, a line of sheathing boards about three feet above the ground was removed from the outside of the building. This provided a place around the outside where the building could be grasped and lifted. Then the troops were lined up around the building, shoulder to shoulder, and told to lift and walk to the designated spot. I participated in this lift and was surprised at how easily we lifted and moved the building.

One evening after we had burned our supply of loose wood, I remembered this old wooden building. We quietly crept out of our hut with bayonets and entrenching tools and made our way to our new-found supply of wood. Our hut was well supplied for a few nights, but soon others in the camp discovered our source of firewood. By early March there was not enough of the building left to make a toothpick. Fortunately, conventional fuel became available again:

> We've got coal again so I guess the camp will not
> be torn down after all. The guys were ripping ev-
> erything up for wood.

The cold winter weather in Korea was made worse by a
lack of adequate shoes, gloves, and clothing. The standard
army issue clothing that was lost with the duffel bags on
the night we arrived was never fully replaced. There was
not enough winter gear, such as warm parkas and insulated shoes, for all of us, so for cold assignments like guard
duty we shared, when possible. However, I remember
many times suffering the cold in ordinary leather combat
boots, wool pants and shirt, and a cheap cotton parka.

The bathing situation was as bad as the food and fuel situations, but not as fundamental to good health and survival.
Nonpotable water was available for bathing. However in
winter, the pipes were frozen and, in warmer weather, water
was often not available because of a break somewhere in
the piping system. We usually used a helmet-full of melted
snow or small amounts of our drinking water for shaving
and for bathing as best we could. Occasionally we would
be recipients of an unexpected supply of wash water:

> The sun is shining here but it is really cold. It
> snowed a little last nite and the wind really blew.
> The 50-gallon oil drums used for fire barrels —
> drums filled with water stored inside (note <u>inside</u>)
> the hut for use in case of fire — are frozen clear to
> the bottom! I had to wait until this afternoon to
> wash myself. The pipes were still frozen, but one
> broke by the mess hall and water is coming out
> there. I went down and got a helmet full, heated it

on the stove, and washed myself. Everybody
washes out of a helmet. I think they are about the
most useful things the army issues. We use our
helmets as basins and cook pots to boil eggs.

Interestingly, some fellows preferred bathing with used
water rather than going to the trouble of fetching their own.
It was not uncommon for one helmet-full of water to be
used by four or five men before being discarded.

We always stood around the pot bellied stove when we
washed. The stove provided a welcome warmth, but it
must also have given some sort of psychological comfort.
Even when we were out of fuel, as was frequently the case,
we would still gather around the stove to wash.

In early summer, all hell broke loose over the lack of bathing facilities. A group of GI's from Michigan wrote a letter
to the *Detroit Times* newspaper to complain about the way
we were living at Camp Hillenmeyer. Their letter was
printed, much to the chagrin of the army. Suddenly, one
day in June or July, a portable shower truck appeared in
camp and we were all ordered to take showers. That was
my first real shower since the salt water one I took on the
Eufaula Victory in December of the previous year. Things
were looking up:

> The shower situation is much better now. We can
> take showers almost any time we want now, be-
> lieve it or not.

Our Michigan buddies served us well, but we were not able
to thank them. They were all identified and transferred to

other posts within Korea. I do not recall ever being told
officially about the transfers, but we were told about the
letter to the *Detroit Times*. We were chided for being com-
plainers and told that we knew things were not that bad.

A few years ago, while reading about Korea and the
American occupation, I thought back to the men who
complained to the *Detroit Times* and wondered what really was their fate. As incredible as it may seem now,
those of us who complained publicly about our depriva-
tions were apparently considered Communists by our
commanding officers.

> ...Major General Orlando Ward reported to Hodge
> that he was looking into 'possible Communist back-
> ground' of soldiers who griped about poor dental
> care, lack of light bulbs, lack of showers, lack of
> brooms, and waiting for months for eye care. These
> '11 sissies' (Ward's phrase) had written to Cecil
> Brown of Columbia Broadcasting System, and
> Brown had aired the complaints. (Smith, page 47.)

Even though our bodies were essentially unwashed, for a
short time after I first arrived in camp we did have clean
clothes. We could take our dirty clothes, along with an
unopened pack of cigarettes, to the supply room. The sergeant would take them to town to some Korean people who
would wash and iron them in return for the cigarettes.

Laundry was washed in a creek by women who placed the
wet clothes on rocks and pounded them with sticks. Thus,
although free of dirt spots, our clothes came back with the
faint smell of sewage that pervaded all of the Korea we

knew. Clothes were ironed with some sort of a sad iron. Once, on a trip to Kunsan, I saw how the Koreans dampened our clothes before ironing them. They would take a mouthful of water and spray it as needed on whatever they were about to iron. They were very expert in spitting out a fine, even spray.

Unfortunately, laundry service became unavailable shortly after I arrived in camp. From then on we were expected to do our own laundry. Soon, the few clothes we had were filthy. Clothes of all types were very scarce; items left unattended, including laundry hung outside to dry, were soon stolen. Shirts, pants, socks, and long underwear were especially prized. Because everybody needed everything, nothing ever dried on a line.

I cannot recall any clothes-washing facilities in camp. The only reference I could find to such in my letters home was a brief one:

> I can't wash up every morning because there usu-
> ally isn't any water in the morning. I admit we are
> a dirty looking bunch of guys but we have no laun-
> dry facilities except GI soap and a brush and you
> can't expect us to be in a hurry to wash our clothes.
> It's an uncomfortable job.

Stealing was a also big deterrent to clothes washing. Why go through the trouble of washing clothes on a concrete floor with a brush, cold water, and GI soap, only to have them stolen while they were drying? When there was fuel for our stoves, we did wash our socks using water or snow heated in a steel helmet on one of the stoves. But even then, we had to keep an eye on them as they dried over the stove.

We never really knew the reason for our shortages of food, clothes, and other items. However, the response from General Witsell to my mother indicated that army commanders at the highest levels in Washington, DC, were not aware of conditions in Korea. I do not doubt that appropriate food and other supplies were shipped from the states, but it is also clear that they did not reach us.

Rumors circulated in camp suggesting that adequate supplies for the army were reaching the port city of Inch'on, but that they were sold or stolen while en route to the infantry units that occupied the southern part of Korea. Strong support for these rumors was the fact that, early in the winter of 1946-47, enlisted men from our infantry units were assigned to guard every freight car that carried army property, including food, on the South Korean railroads.

In 1947, South Korea had few paved roads. Railroads were the primary means of transportation for goods and supplies. Freight trains ran regularly, and included cars carrying military cargo destined for units scattered around Korea. To protect military cargo, the army found it necessary to assign one or two soldiers to ride on each car to protect it from pilferage. I was never assigned to train guard duty. However, those who were told stories of miserable cold and poor food. They would be assigned a loaded freight car at Inch'on, given cases of C-rations and water, and told not to leave the car until it reached its destination. If the car they were guarding was a boxcar, they could ride and sleep inside. If the car happened to be carrying food, they were told they could help themselves. If the car was a flat car or a gondola, they rode and slept outside in the cold.

To reach our area near Kunsan from Inch'on, a distance of about 150 miles, required three to four weeks. Why so long? The guards told us stories of being left alone on side tracks by Korean train crews in the hope that the guards would abandon their cars. The guards learned that they could solve this problem by brandishing their rifles and threatening to shoot the rail crews that tried this trick.

Sometimes the cars were left in the rail yards for days in cities such as Taejon. When this happened, the guards would close the boxcar doors, leaving only about six inches open for ventilation. At night, to defend against bandits who roamed the rail yards, soldiers used their heavy M-1 rifle butts to bash the fingers and hands of those who tried to open the doors further in order to climb inside.

Guards who rode open cars told only of miserably cold rain and wind. Thieves were a lesser problem because open cars carried less attractive goods, such as pipe and lumber.

Interestingly, train guards received no special training and were out of touch with military support for most of the time during their trips. No help was readily available en route because there were few military installations near the railroads. I always felt sorry to see friends leave on these trips, and was always saddened to see how dirty and worn they looked when they returned.

Our superior officers were strangely silent about the whole matter of food and clothing. Camp Hillenmeyer was far down the supply line, and few supplies reached us. Perhaps they had given up trying to cope with what they considered a hopeless situation. Or, perhaps they didn't care. Our commissioned officers seldom saw us, and apparently lived a good life with warm, clean clothes, and an officer's club with good food and plenty of booze. As we often said, "what happened to us was no skin off of their noses."

CHAPTER ELEVEN

A New Assignment: G Company

I enjoyed my job as a lineman, but the work was only part time. We spent almost as much time marching, doing guard duty, cleaning rifles, and general housekeeping, as we did stringing and repairing wires and installing other communications equipment. I had a lot of free time that even volunteering on the switchboard could not fill. My buddies and I felt generally unhappy about being in the infantry because we were not being taught how to defend ourselves.

In light of the unstable situation along the 38th parallel and the stories told by soldiers who had been stationed in the area, we felt that an invasion from the north could occur at any time. We resented the fact that our training never consisted of anything more than marching and guard duty. We were well aware that very few of our vehicles were in running condition. Would our rifles actually fire or were they, like our vehicles, worn out? Where were our officers? They spent almost all of their time in the officers' club and almost no time working with us. How would we protect ourselves, or even survive, if we were invaded from the north?

We discussed these problems at length among ourselves during 1947. We concluded that the U.S. Army's situation was hopeless and, as common soldiers, beyond our ability to fix. Our common sense told us that even though we were more than 100 miles from the 38th parallel, the North Koreans would be upon us in a matter of days.

After being in camp a couple of months I decided to seek a transfer to a unit where, hopefully, I could make more productive use of my time. I went through channels to talk to an officer who was in the 6th Division Engineers. I had seen all the construction that was going on in the camp and decided that I had something to offer. I had worked several summers on a surveying crew in Sonoma County, California. I enjoyed the work, and had learned the basics of surveying during that period. I told the officer about my experience and said that I would like to transfer to his unit. He was very kind to me, and seemed very interested, but that was the last I heard from him.

Despite the fact that there was a large net increase in the population of Camp Hillenmeyer during the first half of 1947, there seemed also to be a fairly large turnover. Whole units and individuals were reassigned and moved out. The individuals who were reassigned usually were sent to work in the Military Government in various towns in South Korea. Military Government jobs were considered plums. The units were usually small, perhaps only four or five men in a town. The job of the Military Government was to coun-

sel mayors and local officials and assist in the establishment of local governments.

GI's assigned to the Military Government were removed
from the strict regimentation and discipline that existed in
the infantry. They had more freedom in their daily lives
than the rest of us. We laughingly joked that the fellows
who left Camp Hillenmeyer for the Military Government
exchanged houseboys for housegirls. What was of real interest to us, though, was that they were said to be better
fed and better quartered than we were.

I knew a few of the fellows who went to military government units. I considered a few of them to be real slobs and
not very bright or motivated. One night, while standing
around the stove with some of my hut mates, I remarked
about one individual who had been transferred out to a
military government unit that very day. I asked out loud
how a guy like that could get such a good job. Some of the
fellows who had been in the army for several years enlight-
ened us.

A high degree of discipline and competence among soldiers was essential for the effectiveness of an infantry unit.
The career of an infantry platoon sergeant, as well as officers on up the line, was dependent on how exemplary a unit
he commanded. Obviously, sergeants wanted privates in
their platoons who followed the rules to the letter, always
marched in perfect formation, snapped to attention at appropriate times, were always neat and clean with never a
hair out of place, and so forth. Any private whose appearance or demeanor detracted from the image of the platoon
and, in turn, his platoon sergeant, was transferred out as

soon as some unit could be found to take him. Conversely, any private who was a credit to his sergeant would never receive a transfer, even if he requested one, because the sergeant had the final say on such matters.

Some of us who had become good friends in the hut listened with great interest to what we were told about who got transferred out and why. Our course of action suddenly became obvious. With inadequate bathing and laundry facilities, it would be very easy to become undesirables. We decided to try to become unacceptable to our sergeants with the hope of being transferred out of the infantry, preferably to the Military Government.

In early March, I began to prepare my parents for my change in attitude:

> I sure won't be worth anything when I get home. I am just like the rest of the guys around here. I do as little work as possible and goldbrick whenever I can.

> There is no use trying to work around here. I worked hard for over two months and didn't get anywhere, so now I am just like the rest. I don't go out of my way to do anything.

> The Memorial Day parade was a success except for our company. We were lousy. You should have seen us making those turns. We looked more like a mob than a formation. Anyway, nobody cared. We all got a big laugh out of it.

The Eufaula Victory, a U.S. Army troop transport. Shown here on December 16, 1946, in San Francisco Bay while departing for Inch'on, Korea, with 1700 soldiers, including the author.

Main deck of the Eufaula Victory with soldiers en route to Korea. Author in foreground.

Entrance to cave, part of Japanese fortification on mountain near Kunsan,
Korea.

Koreans living in abandoned Japanese
cave fortifications near Kunsan.

Korean families sifting through army
garbage. Taken by author after hauling
garbage from mess hall to dump.

Korean women washing clothes in creek.

Road to Kunsan.

Korean men posed for author on road entering Kunsan.

Street in downtown Kunsan.

Residential area on outskirts of Kunsan.

(Above and below) Korean farmers, families, and farm house. The Korean word for child was "aggy".

Farming village on road to Kunsan.

Korean children who came into camp to sell trinkets/

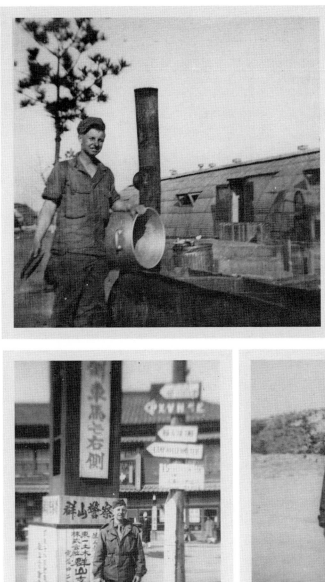

The author on KP in early 1947.

The author at the main crossroads in Kunsan in early 1947.

The author in late spring, 1947. Note the condition of clothing.

KP in early 1947. (Left to Right) Walker, Prinzo, and author. Note Prinzo holding chinaware for exclusive use of officers.

(Above) Author, early 1947 with borrowed parka returning from guard duty.

(Above) Author guarding ammo dump, January, 1947.

(Left) Paul Ginkel, Erie, PA, driver of army six-by-six dump truck and member of the 508th Engineer Utility Detachment, 63rd Infantry Regiment.

(Right) Korean laborers digging drainage ditch at Camp Hillenmeyer.

(Left) Korean construction workers. Note the Korean carrying device known as a "chigeh."

(Left) Shimbu Theater, Camp Hillenmeyer, built by the 508th E.U.D. and Korean construction workers.

(Right) Former Japanese airplane hangar used as beer hall for enlisted men. Known as the Snake Ranch or IP.

(Left) The 508th Engineer Utility Detatchment in fall of 1947. Back row, left to right: J.D. Pauley (WA), Frank Pace (NY), Robert Piazza (MA), Harold Case (OK), Unidentified, Ray Staats (WI), Author (CA), Encil Mills (OH). Front row: Unidentified, Charles Winton (TX), Robert Foster (OH), Kev Noonan (Ontario, Canada), John Carroll (PA), Keith Powell (AR).

Santa Rosa Junior College buddies in 1947. (Top photo front row, left to right) Bill Brandt, Bob Larson, and George Doka in Yokohama, Japan; (bottom, left) Parker Hall in Kyoto, Japan; (bottom, right) the author in Camp Hillenmeyer, Korea. (Left and top photographs provided by George Doka).

(Left) Homeward bound at First Replacement Depot, Yongdungp'o, February 1948, after waiting outside all night. Japanese barracks in background.

(Right) U.S. Army Transport General Haan, waiting in deep water outside Inch'on, February 1948.

(Left) Golden Gate Bridge. Entering San Francisco Bay, March 1948. Photo taken from the General Haan.

In contrast, the men of K Company, who lived nearby, would make the most particular drill sergeant proud. It was a pleasure to watch them march. They practiced a lot and were really good. It was always fun to watch and listen to them. They marched in cadence so perfectly that even the sounds of their squeaking shoes were in perfect timing.

The lack of professional barbers added to our less than neat appearance. When Koreans were employed by the army, a Korean barber would come periodically with his bag of barber tools to cut hair in exchange for a pack of cigarettes.

After the Koreans were gone from camp, volunteer barbers were sought by the camp administration and provided with scissors, clippers, and combs. There was no charge that I recall, and I do not know what compensation the camp barbers received. Needless to say there was a notable lack of quality control:

> Mom, you said to get a haircut. I'll do the closest thing I can to it and let the guy that calls himself a barber butcher my hair up. I think he used to shear sheep before he got in the army.

The camp's inferior barber service was probably responsible for one of our acts of defiance. In any event, it got us into more trouble than we bargained for. We decided to shave our heads. I do not recall what prompted us to cut off all our hair, but I do remember thinking that a bald head would look neater than one with the usual moth-eaten appearance:

I guess the biggest news is I got all my hair cut off. Three other guys and I were sitting around the other nite talking and somehow the conversation drifted to cutting hair. After that it was only a matter of seconds before somebody found scissors and clippers. Carris, Kennedy, Fredricks and I got our hair cut off first, just as we had planned. We looked so silly with our hair cut off that about half of the platoon decided to do the same thing. We couldn't cut hair fast enough. I had a swell time cutting hair.

After about 10 haircuts the lights went out but that didn't stop us a bit. We kept right on cutting by flashlight. It got so afterward that we were giving haircuts whether guys wanted them or not. So the guys that really didn't want haircuts had to run for their lives and not come back until after lights out.

The next day, when our sergeants saw our bald heads they were very angry. They said that shaving our heads was not a decision for us to make. We should have asked permission, and then would have been told that the army does not approved of shaved heads. We were a disgrace to the infantry, but we were secretly pleased that we had earned a few more demerits.

I am surprised that I wrote so much in letters home about our shenanigans. I am sure such letters did not make my mother happy:

It's hard to explain how the morale is around here. We move around like a bunch of snails. Nobody cares if they pass inspection or not. They don't care

if their clothes are clean or dirty, torn, too big or
small. No matter what happens, nobody cares.

Every nite we get bawled out for talking after 'lights
out' (10 PM) and every nite the talking goes on just
the same. The sergeant cusses at us and says he's
going to make us run around the airfield all nite if
we don't shut up. Things quiet down after that,
but the next nite the same thing happens all over
again. I have never seen such an indifferent bunch
of fellows.

We all received KP numerous times and made many a run
around the airfield as punishment for our intransigence.
Fortunately, I made Private First Class (an added stripe and
six dollars more a month) a few weeks before we embarked
on our plan of calculated sloppiness.

I assume our plan of being undesirable worked, but I did
not confess it in letters home. It seemed to me to be too
much of a coincidence that, in late March, shortly after we
implemented our plan, I received a transfer. It was not to
the Military Government, but it was better than nothing.
It seems my abilities as a survey crew member in civilian
life, that I had mentioned to the officer in Division Engineers, were suddenly recognized and I received a new assignment.

An accident of fate dictated that the Wire Platoon of Headquarters Company, 3rd Battalion, 63rd Infantry Regiment,
6th Division became my first assignment. Transfer out of
the infantry to my next assignment was the result of what
might be called calculated incompetence.

My duties in the Wire Platoon ended in late March, 1947, when I was transferred to a surveying party. I wrote home about my new job:

> I've got a new job now. I'm still in the same company, but I am on special duty detailed to post utilities. I'll tell you how I happened to get over there.

> It seems that they are very short of men that know anything about surveying so in order to find some they checked our records and I think I was the only one they found. So they just told me I was working at post utilities in the future.

> Right now a 2nd Lt. and I are the complete survey party. The only instrument we have is a level. Yesterday and today we laid out a new building and leveled the 4 corners.

> We have a lot more work to do also. A bench mark has to be established at the base of the flagpole. We'll do that by running levels from a Japanese barracks on the far edge of the air field. We also have to set the grades for about 6 drainage ditches here in camp. I guess I'll be working there for a couple of months at least.

My new assignment in the engineering section brought me my first real contact with commissioned officers and with Korean laborers. I was very impressed with what hard workers the Koreans were. I was also pleasantly surprised to find that the officers in Engineers were apparently very different from those we had in the infantry:

Mom, you asked if the officers were nice. They are
O.K. as long as they mind their own business. And
they do. We only see our company officers when it
is absolutely necessary. The only officers who earn
their board are the Engineers. They are also the
only ones that don't think they are better than the
rest of us.

My first jobs with the Engineers involved a lot of ditch digging. I did the surveying and then supervised a crew of
Korean laborers who did most of the backbreaking work. I
also had the job of overseeing some Korean contractors who
were hired to build a new theater. Working with the Koreans was really quite an experience:

I wouldn't exactly say I was working as there were
Koreans doing all the work. All I did was tell them
what to do. They're really hard workers — 2 Koreans can do as much as 4 GI's. There is a slight draw-
back though. That is trying to make yourself understood to the Koreans. You ought to see me making all kinds of motions, talking 'baby talk" and
drawing pictures. Here are a few of words I use:
hubba hubba (hurry up); edewah (come here); number 1 (very good); number 10 (lousy); chop chop
(eat); cah or cashu (get out).

Work with the engineering section kept my days busy, but
I still lived in the same hut with the fellows in the wire
platoon. Also, I was still permitted to visit the radio shack
as often as I had time. I really enjoyed the radio shack with
its short wave radio. It was the only place where we could
get news of the outside world.

Other than my new assignment, life in camp changed little during the next few months. Periodic shortages of food and fuel, power outages, and all of the other usual discomforts continued as before, accompanied by occasional happenings that reinforced our low opinion of army administration competence. I tried to put a good spin on one of the more incomprehensible situations that occurred in late April:

> Everybody in the company now has a steel bed. We all got issued them today. I sure am glad to get rid of that cot.

> But, it seems like we jump out of the frying pan into the fire around here. We got steel beds with no mattresses, so now instead of sleeping on canvas we sleep on springs. It's a good thing I can sleep anywhere.

We did the same with our mattressless beds as we did with our cots. We folded our comforters and used them as mattresses. With the cots, a cushion was essential to protect against the cold. With the steel beds, a cushion was essential to protect us not only from the cold but also from the springs. Using our comforters under us left us with three wool blankets. During the cold weather, we tried to make up for the loss of extra cover by sleeping in our clothes.

To add insult to injury, we were issued sheets a month later, but still no mattresses:

> I put sheets on my bed today. That's really 'class.' It's the first time I've had sheets since I left home in

December. I still haven't got a mattress but I'm using 2 comforters in place of one so things aren't too bad. Before we had sheets we used to sleep in a comforter wrapped around us like a jelly roll. It wasn't bad except for the stink.

We still don't have mattresses and we probably won't get any for another six months. I don't care. I sleep just as sound on springs as I ever did. Trifles like that don't bother me anymore.

I apparently was as resigned to a lack of footwear as I was to my lack of a mattress. On May 24, I wrote:

I wore out all my boots including one pair I got issued here. I have one pair which are worn out, but I still have to wear them because they haven't got any new ones. Practically everyone is in the same fix. I guess we'll get shoes someday. It doesn't worry me anyway. It's up to the big shots to be worried about stuff like that. Anyway, if I don't get a pair in the next 2 weeks I'll be quartered and won't have to do anything but eat and sleep until they get me some shoes.

Two weeks later:

I'm laying around the barracks now doing nothing today. I turned my shoes in this morning and now I'm without footwear. All I have is a pair of Korean straw sandals.I really must be hard on shoes as I have worn out 4 pairs in 8 months. Right now the 63rd Inf. is all out of shoes so I guess I'll just

have to wait until some shoes come in. I need the
rest anyway.

And another two weeks later:

Don't send me any shoes. The place is so muddy
when it rains that civilian shoes are useless. Anyway, the army is supposed to furnish shoes. If I
run out of shoes all I have to do is stay in the barracks until they get me a pair. I guess I told you
that I wore out my last pair of shoes and the supply room didn't have anymore. I just stayed in the
barracks 3 days. All I did was go to chow. After 3
days they found me a pair of shoes so I'm getting
around again. That's the only way to get anything
in the army. If I had kept on wearing my old shoes
or worn civilian shoes they still wouldn't have
found me a pair.

Toward the end of June more supplies arrived, including
our summer uniforms:

I got another pair of boots the other day so I think I
will be with footwear for a while now. Also the
supply room got some suntans of the usual sizes
— 48 and midget. So about $1/4$ of the company
doesn't have suntans, me included. We'll probably
get them next winter.

The same thing happened with snowpacks. Snowpacks are extra warm shoes for cold weather. My
feet froze all winter in combat boots. Finally, in
March, when the cold weather was over we got

issued cold weather shoes. What an army. It's a
good thing trifles don't bother me.

In late June I was transferred to G Company. The transfer
to G Company involved only a change in living quarters.
My work assignment remained the same. The transfer was
an unexpected and unhappy one:

> I'm now in Company G of the 2nd Battalion instead
> of Hq third. The 3rd Battalion is being eliminated
> and the guys in it have been sent to about 5 differ-
> ent companies.

> About 10 of us from Hq came to G Company. Some
> went to M, K, I, Mosquito Control, & Regimental
> Hq Co. The ones that went to M, K, & I are lucky
> because these companies are being sent to Inch'on
> and ASCOM City as replacements for the QMs &
> Eng'rs. I call them lucky because they are getting a
> change of scenery. Actually the QMs are going to
> unload ships and the Engineers might be a pick and
> shovel outfit.

> After living together for 5 months the army splits
> us up overnight. I really hated to leave my bud-
> dies. So did the other guys.

> The reason I didn't write last week was because I
> was busy moving to G Company. On top of that I
> was mad because I couldn't leave here with the
> third Battalion. I didn't have a thing to do with the
> transfer. I woke up one morning and they told me
> I was in G Company. The same thing happened to

about 12 other guys from Hq Co. They also were
very mad but couldn't do a thing about it.

ASCOM City, mentioned in my letter, was an acronym for
Army Service Command City. The city was a former Japanese arsenal area west of Seoul that had been taken over
by United States forces on September 16, 1945. ASCOM
City served as an army supply center while American forces
occupied South Korea. In the period between mid-1949,
when the last American forces were withdrawn, and June
1950, the start of the Korean war, ASCOM City was used
by the American Military Advisory Group in Korea and by
the South Korean Army (Sawyer, page 43).

As is typical of youth, within a few days my anger at the
transfer of my friends softened and my memory blurred:

> I'm all settled in G Co now and have made a lot
> more friends. I found out what happened to the
> guys that left here with the 3rd Bn. 75 got picked
> right away for permanent guard duty. I sure did
> miss the guys from Hq Co for a while. After about
> 2 days here in G Co I got to know the guys here
> and forgot all about my old Co. It sure isn't long
> around here before you get to know the guys that
> sleep around you.

G Company was an infantry rifle company. Those of us
who worked for the Post Engineers occupied about half of
a Quonset hut. The other half was occupied by infantrymen whose total activity consisted of marching and guard
duty. They had done nothing else for the past six months

and had nothing else to look forward to for the next eight to ten months.

The infantrymen in our hut were very much like those of us assigned to the Engineers. They had enlisted at about the same time and for the same reason. They wanted to qualify for the GI Bill in order to go to college. But their daily routine, with no opportunity to use their hands or their minds in some constructive activity, not even effective infantry training, was taking its toll.

G Company was what we called a real mess. Most of the men drank to excess every night at the beer hall. They carved initials on one another's chests with bayonets and pocket knives. And one night, after much drinking, they got into a major brawl with neighboring F Company. Several noncommissioned officers who tried to break up the fight were injured. Finally, the men of E Company were called out to quell the disturbance.

I left G Company after a short while, but I often wondered why all of this demoralization was allowed to happen to these young American men who, basically, were not a bad lot. This question was particularly relevant in light of the great needs of the local Korean population. Certainly the men of G Company, and others like them, could have been used in some way to help the Korean people recover from their long occupation by the Japanese military.

My days continued to be occupied with surveying, supervising Korean laborers, and checking on contractors. Part of the work I especially enjoyed was riding the trucks:

I usually have 2 or 3 trucks dispatched to me every day for hauling lumber, cement, and sand. The Koreans do all the work and once in a while I ride around with the trucks when I'm not doing anything else. That's how I do all my riding around. I go to Kunsan with the lumber truck or down to the beach for sand. It's fun for a while, but it's getting monotonous.

The work was not only monotonous at times, but often very frustrating. Frequently, we would arrive at a work site to find that all of the stakes we had set the day before to establish survey points were missing. Somebody had stolen them the night before, probably for firewood.

We also had a lot of difficulties when building the new theater. It was to be located in a field across from the beer hall, and happened to lay in a straight path between the beer hall and the living quarters. We had to reset the stakes and strings that marked the foundation every day because every night the fellows leaving the beer hall would trip over them on their way home in the dark and tear them out.

For some reason, as the work progressed, the fellows never learned to walk around the building site at night. They would just fall over the strings and into the excavation trench that was being dug, pick themselves up, and amble home. Fortunately, as far as we knew, there were never any injuries.

Lieutenant Gonzalez, the officer I worked for, was a very serious young man who had recently graduated from college as a civil engineer. I think he came into the army from the ROTC. He seemed to be very competent, but probably was not given much responsibility and merely followed orders as I did. I liked working for him.

A large part of our work was building drainage ditches. The ditch work was probably in preparation for the coming monsoon season. Because I did most of the surveying, I said a little prayer every night that I had done my job right and when the monsoon rains came the water would run in the ditches as it was supposed to do.

In addition to setting the grade (slope) for these ditches with the army-issued surveyor's level, I also had to establish the line for them. That is, I had to mark the exact locations for their excavation and later construction of their concrete forms. To do this job, I told the lieutenant I needed a transit. A few days later I was told to go to Kunsan and pick up the only surveyor's transit in South Korea. It had been captured from the Japanese sometime earlier by a unit of the 6th Division.

I recall that when I first picked up the transit, it was in what looked like a standard wooden transit box, with a door on the front of the box. In America, such boxes are built in a way that the transit can be secured to the bottom of the box during transport. In any event, having looked inside the box to assure myself that I had been given the correct instrument, I jumped into the right hand seat of the GI dump truck that brought me to Kunsan and cradled the box in my lap for the rough nine miles back to Camp Hillenmeyer.

On arrival back at camp, I turned and leaned outward to step down out of the truck. To my surprise, the door of the transit box opened and the valuable instrument fell out and upside down into the soft ground below. I immediately picked it up. To my great relief, it was not broken. The lenses were clean and the transit appeared to be in good working condition.

When the rains came, I checked the ditches, and they worked perfectly. The water drained as we had planned. However, as I was checking, I noticed that the line of several of the now-permanent concrete ditches was not perfect. They had slight bends in the center. This was not noticeable from the ground by a casual observer. However, because these ditches were big and very long, I am sure that, if they are still in existence, their imperfections can be seen from the moon.

The problem with the alignment of the ditches continued to puzzle me, so after I returned to Santa Rosa I related the story to my friends in the surveying profession. They explained that the main shaft that forms the axis for the vertical motion of the transit telescope was probably bent slightly when the transit fell from the truck, which could account for the bends in the ditches. They also described a simple test that is done regularly in the field to check for and correct such a problem.

Unfortunately, I did not know how to make this correction when I surveyed the ditches. Even so, I will always be indebted to my kind surveyor friends who taught me enough in two summers to enable me not only escape the infantry, but also to perform some useful work during my army service.

I kept asking the Koreans who worked for me when the monsoon would start. Their answer was always an invariable, "Soon." By April the weather was warming and a light rain fell almost every day. The temperature remained comfortable for the next two months, but the rains were gradually increasing in duration and intensity. On June 30, I wrote:

> Don't worry about the weather being too warm. The hot weather isn't due until August.
>
> You think it rains hard in Calif. You ought to see it here. At least 12 inches fell yesterday. It's a good thing we have a good hut. There was only about an inch of water on the floor, so we have no trouble getting around the hut with our overshoes on.
>
> You ought to see the roads around here. You couldn't even get started with a civilian car. These army vehicles are really good. They'll do everything but swim. You ought to see where we go, thru ditches in water up to the seats. They are really rugged.

In the early part of July the weather began to become unpredictable. One day would be sunny and warm and the next overcast and sultry. On other days it would rain heavily. Our suspicions that we had a leaky hut were confirmed:

> Today it is raining like mad. The roof of this Quonset hut leaks like a sieve so there are puddles of

water all over the floor. If this rain keeps up we will probably be floating around in here before morning.

Our problems with the leaky roof were solved a few days later by a move to another Quonset hut. The move was not to spare us from the leaky roof, but rather to bring those of us assigned to special duty together in one unit.

CHAPTER TWELVE

SPECIAL DUTY PLATOON

On July 10, 1947, all of the GI's from G Company and elsewhere in the camp who had been working for the Post Engineers were organized into a Special Duty Platoon and moved to one Quonset hut within G Company. The group included truck drivers, heavy equipment operators, carpenters, electricians, and others like myself with construction skills. Those of us who worked together now lived together. We were a more distinct unit with added duties commensurate with our new status. One of the new duties that was rotated among us was to serve as Charge of Quarters at the office and shop of the Post Engineers.

My first and only typewritten letter home was written from the Post Engineers' office on July 12:

> I guess you are wondering where I got the typewriter. I am just borrowing it. I'm on C.Q. at the Double Hangars tonight and as there are 3 or 4 typewriters in here I may as well use one of them. You must be wondering what C.Q. is. It means Charge

of Quarters. Most of the offices in the camp have to have somebody around at nite to answer the phone and watch the place in general. The person who stays in the office at nite is called a C.Q.

The Double Hangars are 2 great big Japanese hangars that house all the Post Engineers' equipment and offices. Every nite 2 guys have to sleep here. They are picked from a roster of all the guys that work here. That means I'll have to pull C.Q. about once a month. It isn't bad at all, in fact I enjoy it. There is nobody around here — I have the whole place to myself, except for Wild who is on with me.

Things are pretty dull around here. The most exciting thing that happened today was the weather. It rained.

I was going to go on a Red Cross sight seeing tour of a silver smelter that is located in Kunsan, but the rain interfered so another weekend is shot.

In early summer it became obvious that more GI's were leaving Camp Hillenmeyer than were arriving. Some were transferred to other duties in Korea and others were discharged after completing their enlistments, but there were no replacements. At the same time, the last of the draftees, many with as little as seven months of service, were sent home and released from the army.

Interestingly, at the time, we had no idea that many of the draftees would be redrafted within a few years to serve in the Korean War. In fact, no soldier, draftee or enlisted man, who had spent less than 12 months overseas or less than three years in the service was exempt from the draft during the Korean War.

There was no official word about why the shift in population at Camp Hillenmeyer was taking place. I was puzzled by the change, and mentioned it often in my letters:

> I don't know what's going to come off next. All ratings have been frozen and there is a rumor that the 2nd Bn is going to leave. I have given up trying to figure out what's happening as I am always wrong.

> The population of this camp is getting smaller every day. Guys keep going home and we never get replacements. Due to the shortage of men we special duty guys now have to pull guard duty 3 times a month.

The population decline continued for the balance of my tour in Korea:

> The guys that came in the army in June are leaving this camp on Sept 30 and the 1st and 2nd of Oct. No replacements have come in yet but guys keep going home. It won't be long before this place is empty. Nothing is crowded anymore. By the time I leave I doubt if there will be anybody left here to drive us to the railroad station.

Despite the decreasing population, the building and expansion of camp facilities continued unabated. However, we

did not consider it a contradiction, because the decline was
due primarily to discharge of draftees. Much of the construction was to serve the housing and other needs of more
permanent residents, the career commissioned officers and
higher level noncommissioned officers. One such need was
the new theater that our group built with the help of Korean contractors:

> The new theater I told you about is almost finished.
> There is going to be a U.S.O. show in it August 8th.
> It's really a beautiful place, although it's a little
> small, only holds 500. But it is really nice, and when
> I am in there I think I'm in the states. It cost over a
> million yen in labor alone. That's about $750 Ameri-
> can money by my way of figuring. 75¢ is equal to
> about 1000 yen.

Work on a new air field began as the work on the theater
was completed:

> I ran some profile strips for the new airstrip that is
> going to be built here. It's going to be big enough
> to accommodate 4-motored planes. I don't know
> what they are going to build it with as there are
> only 6 dump trucks here. I guess the Koreans will
> build it by hand.

The airstrip originally had been built by the Japanese military, and named the Kunsan Airdrome. The airstrip was
about 5000 feet long and ran roughly parallel with the shore
of the Yellow Sea, which was about one half mile to the
west. The strip was not paved, but had a sod (grass) surface.

Based on test holes that we dug, it appeared to have been carefully built. About three inches of topsoil had been placed on a deep bed of clean, packed sand. Some of the local Korean workers told us that the area had been a mud flat on the shore of the Yellow Sea and that the whole area upon which the airfield and Camp Hillenmeyer stood had been filled in using hand labor.

Nothing was done to improve the airstrip during my stay in Korea. It was used once or twice a month by army spotter planes (similar to Piper Cubs) that usually carried some important military passenger.

United States military history indicates that, during the Korean War, Camp Hillenmeyer was occupied by North Korean troops from July through October, 1950. After the North Koreans were driven out, United States forces increased the length of the airstrip to 9000 feet and built taxi ways and parking aprons as part of the Korean War effort. By the time that war ended, Camp Hillenmeyer was known as Kunsan Air Base, and was capable of supporting both bomber and fighter squadrons.

Today, Kunsan Air Base is a major United States Air Force Base, with concrete runways, passenger terminal, fueling facilities, and accommodations for a large number of aircraft and military personnel — and the road to Kunsan has probably been paved. The old Camp Hillenmeyer may no longer be recognizable.

During the summer of 1947, we worked on numerous other projects in addition to the theater. We built new company shower rooms and latrines, a new enlisted men's club which replaced the old beer hall in the Japanese hangar, and many drainage ditches throughout the camp. While these jobs were in progress, the dependent housing units I had worked on earlier were nearing completion, as reported on the first page of the July 31, 1947, edition of the camp newspaper *Sightseer*:

> Area Engineer Karl C. Lutz said today that thirty new dependent homes will be completed by August 15 'unless unforeseen difficulties present themselves.' About ten of these homes are 85 per cent complete; the remainder of them are in the 75 per cent stage.

> When completed, the houses will be both simple and peaceful. They will be warm in the coldest months since every home will be insulated top, sides and bottom and each room will be equipped with a stove.

> Despite the torrential rainfalls, work on the water and sewage systems has been progressing rapidly.

There not only were torrential rains, but the weather had become very hot and humid:

> The weather during the last few days has been hot with the sun not shining. I guess you call it sultry. It really is sticky. It's getting so I have to change my sox once a week (hah).

> The weather is getting hotter & hotter. About every other day it rains and all the time it's too warm.

I've been sleeping lately with no covers at all, just a mosquito net. The weather is the same here as it was when I was in Guam last December.

It's not only hot but it is also really damp. Everybody's envelopes have sealed themselves, and the stamps are all stuck together. It's practically impossible to keep any gummed paper from sticking together.

When my stamps became stuck together in damp weather, I sent letters free. The free mail privilege for servicemen and women during World War II was still available to us in Korea. However, we were encouraged to use airmail stamps because, we were told, free mail went by ship and took months to reach the States. Being the skeptic I was, I asked my mother whether free letters took longer to reach home than stamped letters. Her reply that there was no difference confirmed my suspicion that all mail was sent out by air. Regardless, my mother kept me amply supplied with six cent airmail stamps.

Letters and newspaper clippings from home were our major sources of information about events in Korea:

When you write include some of the latest world news as we get next to none around here. All we get is army news from 'Stars and Stripes.'

Do you hear anything about the army leaving Korea, over the radio or in the newspaper? Watch the papers for news about Korea. I'd like to know what's going on around here.

It was obvious from the letters I received that stateside news media were reporting much more of the troubles and unrest in Korea than we learned of in camp:

> I didn't know that any Russians were killed in the U.S. Zone until you sent me that clipping. It seems that radio programs beamed this way leave out news about Korea. Also the 'Stars & Stripes,' which is three days old when we get it, is conspicuous with its shortage of news about Korea.

My letters home frequently contained assurances that I was safe that only could have been in response to concerns of my parents:

> You seem worried about me being in danger. There is nothing to worry about as we are a long way from the Russian front. The camp is well guarded nite and day. It's just a matter of time before I will be home again, that is if the Russians don't start anything. Don't worry about riots. We didn't have any around here. The part of Korea that I'm in is very quiet. Whenever there is trouble, it's around Seoul.

Despite my desire to keep my mother from worrying about my safety, I unthinkingly reported every episode that could have given her additional cause for concern:

> We had an alert the other day and expected some trouble from the Koreans. Nothing happened and everything is cooled off now. The trouble was the

Koreans fighting among themselves. A mob tore up a Communist newspaper office in town.

Unknown to the rank and file in the camp, the headquarters command must have been concerned that local unrest might reach the camp. In mid-August, shortly after I moved to G Company, we had a practice alert:

I guess you read in the newspapers that the army in Korea was alerted. I'll tell you how it affected me.

It was Sunday morning. At 6 AM I got off guard duty (3rd relief), took off my shoes and went to sleep. I slept about 5 minutes when they woke us up and told us to go eat chow. After chow they told us we had five minutes to fall out with light pack, raincoat, mess gear, steel helmet, gas mask, rifle, entrenching tool, bayonet, and canteen of water. We fell out and piled in trucks and drove as far as the edge of camp. Then we turned around and they drove us back to the company.

We all thought something was going to happen as everyone had to go, Special Duty, office workers & even the bugler. Everyone was excited and hoping it was a riot as it would break the monotony of this place. Anyway nothing happened. It was just a dry run. Everything was over by 9 AM.

I added the following cryptic note that stirs my curiosity, but whose meaning is completely lost to me now:

I'm enclosing a clipping from the 'Stars & Stripes,' the newspaper we get over here. Don't take the article too seriously as this paper is always exaggerating.

In my next letter I sent a news item, the source of which I did not identify, along with a personal response that I would echo today:

Did you read about those 3 Americans that got captured by the Russians? In case you didn't know, they were returned in 2 weeks alive and well. I guess the Russians don't want a war yet.

I'm sure glad I'm in the 6th instead of the 7th Division. If I had gone to the 7th, I probably would be pulling guard duty along the 38th Parallel, which isn't such a good deal — so I hear.

Life in the G Company Special Duty Platoon continued along with little change from prior months, with the exception that shortages of heating fuel were of no concern and cold water showers were welcomed and refreshing because the weather was so warm.

The electric power supply became more and more unreliable until, by late summer, it stopped completely. The only electric power available after that time was for essential uses only, and was provided by portable diesel generators. Thus, only the hospital, headquarters installations, and the shop area of the Post Engineers had electricity. The remainder of the camp was simply left dark.

Supplies of all sorts were still short. Sometime in late summer it became obvious that, for some reason, considerable amounts of our food and clothing were coming from Australia:

> I got issued a pair of Australian shoes the other day. They really are clodhoppers. I wouldn't wear them to a dogfight. I think if it wasn't for Australia we would be barefooted and starved out by now. An awful lot of our supplies come from Australia.

Interestingly, many of the supplies from Australia were of very good quality. Their wool trousers that were issued to us during our second winter were thicker and warmer than comparable army-issue trousers. Also, the butter and fruit preserves were of excellent quality.

Despite the supplies from Australia, shortages of clothing were the rule during my entire time at Camp Hillenmeyer. Worn out shirts, pants, and other articles of clothing that were shipped to the motor pool for use as wiping rags were often in better condition than the clothes we were wearing. These rags arrived at the motor pool in large bales, like hay. Each piece of clothing was stenciled with a large X, which meant that it was Class X clothing intended for use as rags.

We made a fine looking group wearing tattered and torn clothing stenciled with large X's. Curiously, no one in authority ever said a word about the condition of our clothing. The arrival of a bale of Class X items was something to write home about:

We got some new clothes today. A whole bunch of worn out clothes came in the motor pool for grease rags. Instead everybody dived for them to wear. Our clothes are all wearing out and we never see any new ones. It's a good thing I'm coming home pretty soon as my clothes won't hold out much longer.

Before the summer was over, I was reassigned for the last time during my tour in South Korea.

CHAPTER THIRTEEN

THE 508TH ENGINEER UTILITY DETACHMENT

There was a great deal of excitement in my life the first week of September 1947. I shared the good news with my family:

> A lot has happened in the last few days. First I got transferred to E Company. I moved Friday afternoon into the Special Duty hut in E Company. There isn't much to moving in the army. You turn in your bed, sheets, rifle, and all the heavy stuff. All you take with you are your clothes and personal stuff. When I moved to E Co, I went to the supply room and drew everything I needed except a rifle. That's one thing I like about this company, I don't have a rifle.

> The next event was when I made T/5 a day after I moved in here. I guess you've heard of the rating. I now make $108 a month. I sewed a set of stripes

on my shirt the other day. They look pretty
sharp. Practically all of the guys at P.E. now have
ratings. In the last 2 weeks about 50 guys made
T/5 or corporal.

All of the guys in this hut work at P.E. so I know all
of them. Most of them, at one time or another, lived
in the same hut I did in another company.

The above, written on September 8, was followed the next
day with the really good news:

I moved again yesterday to the 508th Engineer Det.
At last I am out of the Infantry. I hope I can stay
here for a while. The 508th is a pretty small outfit,
32 men to be exact. We live in one Quonset hut at
the end of Hq Co 2nd Bn. It's a good deal, no guard
or KP or anything.

The men of the 508th Engineer Utility Detachment (EUD)
lived in a Quonset hut located in a headquarters company
area of the 2nd Battalion, 63rd Infantry. All of the offices
and equipment of the 508th EUD occupied an old Japanese
airplane hangar and fenced area next to the Service Company of the 63rd Infantry. The Service Company used the
adjacent hangar, exactly the same as that of the 508th, to
house its shops and equipment.

I have no recollection of the 508th EUD being in that hangar when I first arrived in camp. Sometime in the spring of
1947, the nucleus of the 508th EUD, namely my special duty
group, was formed to replace a detachment of the 6th Division Engineers Battalion. Prior to that time, all building

and maintenance of the camp was the responsibility of this detachment, which was stationed somewhere in Kunsan. The change was probably made because the latter were combat engineers and we were no longer at war.

The transfer out of the infantry was something I had wanted for as long as I had been in the army. The infantry was not interesting to me. I did not like the regimentation and the complete lack of respect for the individual soldier. There seemed to be no opportunity to learn anything, not even how to be an effective infantry fighter. Thus, my transfer out of the infantry was very agreeable to me:

> I like it a lot better here in the 508th than I did in G Company. For one thing I don't have a rifle. A rifle is a bother as the climate around here makes them rust overnight. They keep all the rifles in the supply room where one guy takes care of all of them.

> Another thing is the chow. All the meat that was fed in G Company was in the form of stew. Those cooks don't know how to cook anything else. Here in Hq 2nd we have roast, steak, and occasionally stew. Also we have ice cream every day compared to once in 3 months in G Co. I just finished eating noon chow — mashed potatoes, chicken, carrots, bread & fruit salad. The food is good and I'm getting all I can eat.

The person who was in charge of the guns was Hollis Gholston from Gary, Indiana. He was the supply clerk for our hut. He kept all our guns in the back room of our hut, and did a fine job of keeping them cleaned and ready for use. A running joke in the hut was that if Gholston failed to keep the rifles clean and failed to keep our superiors satisfied, we would force him to sleep outside in the cold. He took our foolish teasing with good nature. I was personally very grateful to him because he relieved me of a lot of responsibility. I had no interest in having my own rifle.

Actually, the whole hut was grateful to Gholston, because he took good care of us and kept us well supplied. Whenever the camp scheduled a trip to a supply depot, Gholston would send one of our own drivers and a truck along in the event that some surplus items that would add to the comfort of our lives were available for relocation. Our drivers would claim such items and bring them home before they disappeared into someone else's truck.

On one trip, the drivers brought back a small gasoline-powered generator that seemed to have no claimants. We set it up in the back of our hut where it provided us with welcome light at night. The fact that we had lights every night while all the other huts were in darkness was obvious to all, but then we were engineers so the other GI's thought it not remarkable.

The generator exhaust pipe that exited the rear wall of our hut was remarkable, nonetheless, to an officer who was inspecting the camp one day about a month or so after the generator's installation. The officer investigated further, found our generator, and liberated it. That was the end of night lighting in our hut, but it was the beginning of a brief, uncomfortable period of uncertainty about our future. We were threatened with court-martial, loss of stripes, and whatever other punishment the administration could devise.

I felt very sorry for the senior noncommissioned officer in our hut, Sergeant Jim Fisher, who must have taken most of the blame for our transgression. Jim, a two-year enlistee from Thurmont, Maryland, was the head electrician for the camp. He was a very competent electrician and a really fine person who was very well liked. Fortunately, the whole generator episode was gradually forgotten, and Jim and the rest of us received no lasting scars.

The Engineers were a very close-knit group. Being placed in a unit of our own with no need to play soldier, as we felt we were doing in the infantry, gave us a sense of camaraderie and purpose. For the first time I felt free to do my job without constraints imposed by infantry rules and duties. My work assignments continued unchanged, and expansion of camp facilities progressed without interruption:

> I guess you're wondering what kind of work I'm doing lately. I've been ordering materials for a new day room, 7 new latrines and a concrete drainage ditch. I go to the office every morning, get requisitions for whatever I need and send trucks to Kunsan after it. Then I go around and see that the laborers don't make mistakes.

> I don't know if I mentioned it before when I was working on it, but we have a new snack bar in this camp. It almost resembles a soda fountain at home. All they sell in the place is coke, sandwiches, and one flavor of sundae. It's better than nothing.

The 508th EUD had its own mechanics, electricians, carpenters, and other skilled construction workers. It also had its own heavy equipment, such as dump trucks, bulldozers, graders, scrapers, and the rock crusher at the quarry south of camp. The latter provided gravel for concrete work.

Before the rock crusher was installed in the summer of 1947, the work of making little rocks from big rocks was performed by Korean laborers employed by the army. Army blasting experts would place the dynamite and set it off. The Koreans would then work on the boulders let loose by the blast. It was quite a sight to see a hundred or more Korean men at the quarry chipping away at the big rocks.

The EUD employed many Koreans from Kunsan and surrounding villages. Koreans were employed primarily as laborers, because they had no skills for tasks such as electrical work or heavy equipment operation. One exception was carpentry; some Koreans were excellent carpenters and were employed as such. The majority of Korean employees worked under the supervision of EUD labor foremen.

Expansion and improvement of the facilities continued for the balance of the time I was at Camp Hillenmeyer. The EUD built a potable water system, beginning with a water storage tank on a nearby mountain top to feed the camp by gravity, a system of water-delivery piping, and a water purification plant. Among other additions were new shower rooms for each company, an enlisted men's club, a theater, and a hospital.

The expansion and improvements at Camp Hillenmeyer were probably in preparation for peacetime occupation, because they were accompanied by continued construction of dependent housing units that had been started months before. I remember, from a letter written before I was transferred to the 508th EUD, that I was not impressed with the quality of materials used for the units:

> I worked out at the dependent housing project today laying out 10 new houses. Maybe I should say shacks. They are being built out of Japanese lumber which is of the same caliber as other Japanese material here - not so hot.

Despite my disapproval, the construction of dependent housing seemed to bode well:

> I don't think there is going to be a war because they sure aren't preparing for one. All the big shots are bringing their families over here. They sure wouldn't bring their wives and children here if there was any danger.

Because the group of us who were transferred to the 508th detachment were now separated from the infantry, we no longer had the services of infantry guards. Thus, we had the added duty of protecting our truck drivers. Trucks were sent almost daily to supply warehouses in Kunsan, where a good deal of stealing was taking place. Trucks also went to Kunsan every day to pick up Korean laborers in the morning and return them at night.

By mid-1947, Korean animosity toward American servicemen appeared to be on the increase. Thus, truck drivers were vulnerable to attacks not only from thieves, but also from disgruntled local citizens. We served as armed guards for our drivers on every run they made. One of my first assignments in the 508th E.U.D. was truck guard duty:

> I just got back from riding 'shotgun' on the 'work run.' I'll explain. The work run is about 8 trucks that haul laborers to Kunsan. They are picked up in Kunsan in the morning and brought to camp where they work all day. At night the trucks take them back to town. Every truck that goes on the run has to have 2 guys on it, a driver and anybody else. I was the 'anybody else.'

Although I was pleased that I did not have my own rifle, I did not object to carrying a rifle on truck runs. Just before a run, the shotgun rider picked up a rifle at the supply room and then returned it at the end of the run. However, something that worried me very much was the fact that we were given only one clip, eight bullets, to protect our drivers and ourselves. One clip would have been totally inadequate if we ever ran into any major difficulty.

I rode shotgun only about twice a week, but after a few times it became obvious to me that the truck drivers were quite capable of protecting themselves in most situations. My first experience with trouble while serving as truck guard came after we had taken a group of workers back to Kunsan at the end of a work day. It was just getting dark. We stopped in the center of a muddy dirt street where it was usual to drop off the workers. They all got off the truck, and we began moving slowly away along the muddy street on our way back to camp. Suddenly, some sort of a problem arose on the ground and the Koreans started running after us, shouting and trying to climb back on the truck.

The driver gunned the truck and we sped off. Some Koreans clung to the truck, trying to pull themselves aboard, but as the truck gained speed, they fell away.

I did not have the vaguest idea what the workers' problem was, but if any had gotten back on the truck, I knew my job would be to climb in back and hit them with the butt of my M-1 rifle. There was little other choice. We could not communicate with them because we did not speak their language. There was no help nearby, and to stop the truck would be very dangerous. The truck cab was canvas, not steel, hence any unfriendly individuals in the back of the truck could easily attack us. Fortunately, none of the workers were able to board the truck. I was very relieved that I did not have to use my rifle.

Interestingly, when riding shotgun, we had the choice of carrying an M-1, a big rifle with a heavy wooden stock, or an M-2 carbine, a light rifle about the size and weight of a B-B gun. In all of my guard duty in Korea, including truck guard duty, I always insisted on carrying an M-1 rifle. I had learned in basic training that the M-1, even without ammunition, was a very effective weapon.

The second time there was a problem when I was truck guard was later in the year, during a severe snow storm. Like the first time, I had no idea why the episode occurred. We were using an open dump truck, with a canvas-topped truck cab, to return the laborers to town. About four miles outside of Kunsan, the Korean laborers began cursing us and pounding the canvas cab cover. I looked back but could see no reason for the disturbance. As the Koreans became more active and vocal, the driver turned around and shouted to them to be quiet. As the cursing and pounding increased, the driver slowed the truck and pulled the lever to raise the bed as he would do to dump a load of gravel. The Korean laborers were dumped unceremoniously, cursing and yelling, out onto the snow-covered road as the truck sped off. Again, I was happy that I did not have to fight anyone, and again, I very much regretted that we did not understand the language so that we could know what the Koreans were obviously so very upset about.

The experience of riding shotgun also introduced me to a seamy side of life that was unfamiliar to me. For example, one of our truck drivers who regularly drove to and from Kunsan always seemed to have fewer clothes than the rest of us. He was forever borrowing a shirt or a field jacket from one of us. Finally, when we asked him why he was always borrowing clothes, he laughingly told us that he gave his to a prostitute in exchange for her services during his regular trips to town.

For the major portion of my stay in Korea, particularly while with the Post Engineers, I lived and worked with people who liked to work and wanted to go to school when they got home. There was little interest in prostitutes and none were ever brought into our Quonset hut. I seriously doubt that any of my friends ever partook of such pleasures at some other location in camp or in town.

Actually, the only time I ever saw a prostitute during my stay in Korea was one late winter night while riding shotgun on a post engineer truck. We had delivered a load of Korean laborers to Kunsan and dropped them off on the main street of town as usual. Instead of going around the block and returning directly to camp, the driver headed down toward the port area of Kunsan. It was after dark and I was not sure where he was going, so I asked him. He said he was picking up a prostitute for some friends and that it would only take a few minutes extra.

The driver stopped near a small building, left the engine running, went inside, and immediately returned with a young, small Korean woman. He obviously had done this before and knew what he was doing. He placed her between us on the front seat and drove toward camp. I said, "How are you going to get her through the guard gate." He replied, "Watch me. I'll push her head down under the dashboard just before we get to the gate and we'll roll through as usual." Sure enough, everything went as planned.

Once inside, I asked where he was going to take her. He said, "Over to one of the abandoned Japanese barracks buildings at the north end of the airfield where some friends are waiting." I said no more. Shotgun riders had no authority over truck drivers. Without specific instructions, it was assumed the duty of the shotgun guard was solely to protect the driver. It was no business of a shotgun guard where a driver went or how long he stayed.

The second reason I said nothing was peer pressure. Truck drivers, fellow enlisted men, had to be considered comrades to be protected at all costs. In the absence of instructions to the contrary from a superior, no shotgun guard would have interfered with the business of his driver or reported the driver's action to authorities. Such behavior would have spread through the grapevine and resulted in the shotgun guard being classed as a wise guy who acted without orders against another enlisted man. He would have been shunned by the other enlisted men in the camp.

Acting against other enlisted men was a serious problem for the military police unit in the camp. They had no friends outside their own small group. In one instance that I witnessed, a former member of the military police unit, when transferred to our infantry unit, was thrown out of the hut bodily upon arrival and forced to sleep outside in the snow. The next day he was transferred somewhere else.

By the end of August, the weather began to moderate and the rains lessened in frequency and intensity. By the end of September, it began to cool:

> It will be winter before long around here. Three weeks ago I was sleeping without blankets at all and now I'm using 3. Today is Sunday, the weather is clear and cool. I can look out in back and see the Yellow Sea, which is rougher than usual.

By the end of October we were preparing for winter:
> The weather is getting steadily colder. We got issued Parkas the other day. It won't be long before we really need them. But the weather is still surprising me — it's still comfortable.

In November the winter set in and we had our first snow:

> The weather has taken a cold turn. I finally put on my 'long-johns' the other day. Practically everybody in the hut has them on by now. The morn-

ings are really cold lately and do we hate to get up. We have to fall out for reveille at 6:40 AM so we stay in bed until about 6:35, then get up in a big hurry and barely make it. We got our first snow this morning, about 1/2 inch in all. It was all melted by 3 this afternoon.

My 20th birthday on November 1 was memorable. I wrote to my mother:

> You really have it figured when it comes to sending packages. I received one from you right on my birthday. It had some canned fruit and cookies in it. I also received a 2 lb.. box of MacFarlands candy from Mrs. Hall. I will write her a letter this morning and thank her for it. I had quite a time yesterday. I got about 30 licks from the guys for my birthday. They got me down and gave me a spanking with a board.

Nine days later my brother Bob had a birthday. Bob wrote to me often while I was Korea and even baked cookies for me. Just before his 14th birthday, in a letter thanking him for some books and magazines he sent, I offered him some rather fatherly advice:

> I'm surprised to hear you are going to high school. I'm used to you being a 'little brother'; I guess you are not so little anymore.

> You asked me about joining the French club and a couple of others. By all means do and have a good time. Clubs are good for you as you will meet more

people and have more friends. Have all the fun you can while you are in school because once you're out, you're out. I don't mean to quit studying, you can get good grades and still have a good time. When you're in class stay on the ball, after hours you can take it easy.

Bob was a good student and a hard worker. After high school, he worked his way through college and medical school and became a well-respected orthopedic surgeon.

The population decline in the camp continued at such a pace that by mid-November some facilities began to close:

This camp is getting smaller and smaller everyday when it comes to men. Our mess hall closed up today so now we eat in E Company. A, B & F mess halls are also closed. In about 2 1/2 months this camp will be empty if replacements don't get here pretty soon.

It seems that nobody likes the army. A big recruiting drive has been launched and nobody is reenlisting — just a few of the 20-year men who don't know anything but army.

Three more guys from this hut are going home in a week or so. That will leave 12 of us in this hut. Boy, does it look empty. The other huts in the camp have fewer men than we do. We still aren't pulling guard duty but I imagine we will before very long. Practically everybody else in camp is and they are on guard every other nite. When more guys go

> home they are going to have to get men from some-
> where and I bet they'll get us.

The number of enlisted men in camp toward the end of
1947 was probably not much greater than 200. Those of us
left began to worry about our vulnerability. We knew there
was a great deal of unrest in the local population, which
was further complicated by deteriorating relations between
North Korea and South Korea. The twelve of us left in our
hut often talked among ourselves at the end of a day about
what we would or could do in the event of hostilities.

It was obvious from conversations with soldiers who passed
through Camp Hillenmeyer that the total American force
in South Korea was minimal. The fact that the American
military posture was not in keeping with the usual standards for American military forces was a powerful issue
for us. Even at age 19 or 20, I wondered why the American
Army, facing a tense border situation opposite an unfriendly
power, namely the Soviet Union, was short of men and ill-
equipped, clothed in rags, improperly fed, and not given
battle training. Our general consensus was, in the event of
an invasion from the north, our forces could easily be over-
run. We were very concerned that, in such an event, the
army might simply abandon the few of us still left in camp.
We decided that it would be wise to have an escape route
mapped out and ready to implement in case of emergency.

The idea of taking refuge further south in the country did
not seem reasonable. The roads were dirt and there were
no highway signs or maps. In fact, there were no highways; the only real transportation link was the railroad,
and the nearest station was 30 miles away by dirt road. We

could not communicate with the local people to obtain directions. Even if we could, the local population was, for the most part, an immobile one that knew nothing about what lay on the other side of the nearest hill.

We were aware also that travel by motor vehicle was very difficult. Probably the most extreme situation we knew of was that experienced by a group of soldiers who were assigned to drive a truck along a secondary coastal road from Seoul to Camp Hillenmeyer, a distance of about 150 miles. The trip took almost a month! Their truck got bogged down in muddy roads dozens of times. For want of a good map, they lost their way even more often. And, because the people who lived along the way had never left their home villages, they did not know where their local roads led.

We finally decided that, if we were abandoned, we would take our rifles and one of our trucks and drive to Kunsan harbor. Several of the men in the hut had a cache of ammunition hidden under the floor. I never paid much attention to such things, but was relieved to learn about the store. We were united in our commitment to let no one stand in our way. In Kunsan we would commandeer an ocean going fishing vessel or tug to take us to Japan. Fortunately, we never even came close to the need for testing our plan.

Our expectation that the 508th would eventually be tapped for guard duty finally came to pass. This time, though, conditions on guard duty were quite different from what they were the winter before. Formerly, when possible, a whole company was assigned to guard duty at the same time. In this way, the company could stay in its own living quarters while individuals took turns on the duty shifts.

Now, with all of the companies nearly empty, a few men were taken from each of several companies and housed together for the 24-hour period in a guard house. There we lacked the amenities of our home base.

Men assigned to guard duty would borrow parkas from others in the hut. Every hut had fewer parkas than it had men because of the clothing shortage. Parkas were essential while walking a post to help protect against the cold. They were also essential to protect against the cold in the guard house. The guard house was a Quonset hut with a desk at one end, no bunks, no heat, and a bare light globe hanging from the ceiling. When we came in from our two hours on duty, the only place to rest for the next four hours was the concrete floor.

All of us on the same shift had to rest or sleep fully clothed in one area on the concrete floor so when the time came to go back on duty we could be found. The bare concrete floor was cold and hard and uncomfortable but, for some reason I could not understand, I managed to sleep reasonably well. After four hours of rest, we were wakened with a kick on our feet, a flashlight beam in our eyes, and shouts of, "Time to go, you guys." Guard duty was now a really miserable experience.

By early December 1947, Koreans began returning to the camp to help with housekeeping and maintenance, but there were still certain chores that we were assigned:

> Today I'm fire guard in the hut so I have plenty of time to write. I'll probably send all my Christmas cards today as Christmas is getting pretty close.

I guess you are wondering what a fire guard is. Well, there isn't much to it. Everybody in the hut takes turns at it so we all get a chance to stay inside about once every 12 days. All I do is keep the fires going in the hut so it stays warm all day. The Koreans carry in all the wood & coal and carry out the ashes. After the guys leave in the morning the fire guard sweeps out the hut and straightens the place out — also it is good to have somebody in the hut to keep an eye on things.

Just before Christmas, the number of Koreans working in the camp increased significantly:

There are a lot of Koreans working in camp now — more and more as the GI's go home. There are no replacements coming in so Koreans are working in mess halls (KPs) and laundry. They are even teaching Koreans how to drive trucks.

In the same letter there was a rare outpouring of the bitter feelings that many of us held, particularly toward the officers whom we felt did not suffer the privations we did:

Yesterday we got a big reenlist speech. They touched on every point from patriotism to the money you can make in the army. They promised us everything. However, the guys are wise to that recruiting propaganda. They'll never get me to 're-up.' Even the Regimental Commander Col. Hamilton got up and gave us a sad line. He even wished us a Merry Christmas.

Last year things were different when they knew they had us for another year. They didn't care if we starved or froze as there were a lot of guys around. Now they are giving us a lot of soft soap to try to get us to stay but we haven't forgotten last winter.

I think these big shots around here are beginning to worry they will have pull their own guard duty. They gave us a hard time for a year — now the 'worm is beginning to turn.'

My next letter, several days later, was considerably more cheerful:

Right now we are having Christmas vacation. It started the afternoon of the 23rd and ends Monday the 29th. Everybody is surprised at the length of it; the army doesn't usually give very much time off.

We really have raised the roof around here in the last few days. Wednesday morning we had a big snowball fight inside the hut — what a mess. Then Wednesday afternoon we hauled in a load of beer & coke and whiskey for a party we were supposed to have Xmas day. The guys just couldn't stand to see all that stuff piled up in the barracks so they just had to taste it and before very long they were going full blast.

The guys were roaring around to the other huts and vise versa until midnight. Then we went to mid-

night mass. I guess it was about 4 AM before everybody got to bed.

Yesterday we had a big Christmas dinner with turkey and a lot of other stuff. I think it was better
than Thanksgiving dinner.

Although I never wrote home about it, that dinner on the
earlier holiday, Thanksgiving, was a disaster. Everybody
who ate it got miserably sick, with vomiting and diarrhea.
Fortunately, I missed that particular noontime dinner with
its special turkey and stuffing because several of us had
been called to fix a water main that was leaking; a weld
had cracked open. The repair job took such a long time
that we did not return to the hut until just before supper.
The mess hall was nearly empty that evening when the few
of us who missed the noon festivities went in for our
evening meal. Everyone else was still sick.

I was glad that I had to work that Thanksgiving Day, not
just because I escaped food poisoning, but because work
for me was never a problem. I enjoyed the construction
activities and the company of my fellow engineers very
much, so being called on for extra work never really bothered me.

CHAPTER FOURTEEN

OFF DUTY HOURS

One of the most difficult aspects of my time in Korea was the weariness and lassitude brought on by the prison-like conditions that we had to endure for a prolonged period of time. There was a Spartan daily routine. No one was allowed to leave the camp except on work details. We had no communication from our officers, other than those in the engineers detachment, concerning our goals or purpose. Whatever communication we had was one direction only, from top down. We had no idea of what the military was trying to accomplish in Korea; thus, we had no sense of participation in the mission of the organization. Living at Camp Hillenmeyer gave me the feeling of being locked away in big, cold, gray, empty warehouse in a far-away place.

One of my few pleasures and main diversion while at Camp Hillenmeyer was reading. I could be entertained for hours with a good book, magazine, or newspaper. However, at night, even if we had something to read and time to read, we seldom had light. I frequently mentioned our erratic electricity supply in my letters home. Usually, my comments were openly critical, but in a few letters my references to the lack of lighting seemed to be merely statements of a fact of life:

> I received two letters from home today. One this afternoon and one tonight. I read the one I got tonite by firelight as the electricity was off.

On the rare occasions that we did have sufficient light by which to read, there was usually a lack of reading material. My mother tried her best to keep me supplied with books, magazines, and newspapers, which everyone in our hut appreciated. I made reference to the latter in a letter to my brother:

> I walked in the hut the other day and found a lot of mail waiting for me on my bunk. An airmail package with the Santa Rosa paper in it, another package with magazines, candy, and gum, and two letters — one from you and one from mom, and a postcard from mom. Thanks a lot for the magazines and papers as reading material is scarce around here. Everybody in the hut has asked me for the books when I'm finished.

Many of my letters contained references to receiving and sharing of books and magazines:

> Did I tell you I received your package? It had two boxes of candy and some reading material. Boy, those papers were really swell. I was going mad from lack of something to read. Right now I've got

a new Reader's Digest lined up. I'll get it tomorrow when Dunn finishes it. 'Old' Dunn is about 19 and from Chicago.

I took a lot of pictures in my off duty hours. I tried to record everything about my experience in Korea as best I could. I photographed my buddies, our living quarters, buildings in camp, Korean peasants and workers, their houses, and the scenery in and around camp. Almost all of the film I used was sent to me from home. When I first arrived at Camp Hillenmeyer, I returned film home for developing because I was told that local film developing services were of poor quality. I explained this in a letter of January 20, 1947, ten days after I arrived in camp:

> I'm going to send home an exposed roll of film as soon as I can find something to wrap it up with. I can get the roll developed here by Koreans, but they do a bum job and worse yet, you never get the right pictures back. They always get them mixed up.

Fortunately, I finally decided to trust my own judgment about local film processing capabilities. I informed my parents shortly after the experience:

> I changed my mind and sent my films to a Korean shop in Kunsan. They came out good, as I expected they would. I'm sending the negatives home. You can have some jumbo size pictures made from the negatives. I've got some small size prints here that the Koreans made. I'll send those home, too, with writing on the back of them so you will know where the pictures were taken.

Despite the good quality of local service, I usually sent exposed rolls of film home for developing because it was the less expensive method. Unfortunately, mail service was not always reliable, and occasionally rolls of film were lost en route to California. This prompted me sign up for a course in photography in July 1947:

> There is a school in this camp for guys who want to go. I'm taking a photography course starting Monday. It's from 6 to 7 PM 3 days a week. The main reason I'm taking the course is so that I can develop the pictures I take here. That will save me sending the rolls home undeveloped. On top of that, I might learn something.

My plans were short-lived. Two weeks later I wrote:

> I'm not taking the photography class like I planned. The class fell thru. Not enough guys signed up for the class. The minimum number of guys was 5 and only about 2 signed up. That's the way it is over here. The guys are almost too lazy to go to chow.

Several months later, after our group had completed construction of a new hospital, I found a solution to my problem. On October 26, I wrote:

> I have been developing my own films; I should say trying. We have ruined one roll of film already. I have a buddy in here by the name of Fisher, from Maryland, who knows the guy that runs the x-ray lab at the hospital. We go over there anytime we feel like and use the darkroom. We are getting so

we can make pictures, and when we get some time, I'll make some to send home.

I guess I was not fated to learn about photography. The x-ray laboratory and its darkroom, along with the rest of the hospital, was destroyed by fire shortly after the complex was completed.

The photography class was not my only frustrated effort at education while at Camp Hillenmeyer. Within a few days after arrival in camp I learned of the U.S. Armed Forces Institute (USAFI):

> I went over to Special Services yesterday and found out about a USAFI course. I'm going to take some subjects as soon as they get some application blanks, which will be next week.

A week later:

> I'm still trying to take that USAFI course. I was over at I&E (Information & Education) yesterday again. I have to go back again next Wednesday because the guy there Saturday didn't quite know what was going on. Anything that has to do with the army sure has miles of red tape attached.

And the next week:

> Things are pretty dull around here. There's absolutely nothing to do in off duty hours. I'll be glad when my USAFI course gets here. I just sent my application for it to Tokio [sic] a few minutes ago.

It costs $2 to enroll; after that I can take all the courses I want free.

A month later there was a post script to my letter home, "P.S. I got my USAFI course yesterday."

The course I had enrolled in was a mathematics course called integral calculus. I had already taken differential calculus at Santa Rosa Junior College. The material I received was a text book with a few instructions. I studied the book and worked the problems, and then waited for further material and instructions. I assumed that what I had received was a first lesson of a correspondence course, but nothing further ever came. Perhaps follow-up materials were lost in the mail. I did not pursue the matter.

Many of my off duty hours were spent in housekeeping chores such as straightening my bunk area, washing clothes, and polishing shoes. After long hours of guard duty, my off hours were spent catching up on my sleep.

During off duty hours in the latter months of my tour in Korea, I frequently volunteered to ride shotgun on the engineer trucks that transported Korean workers between Kunsan and Camp Hillenmeyer. These were 2 1/2-ton dump trucks, also called six-by-sixes. Sometimes I would go on an evening run just for the ride:

The guy that sleeps next to me here in the 508th is a truck driver on the run (to Kunsan) so I ride with him once in a while. About 3 or 4 guys in the hut go every night on different trucks for the fun of it. Anything to break the monotony.

Several letters latter I identified my bunk neighbor:

> I rode into town yesterday afternoon with a driver
> that sleeps next to me. He's from Ohio; name is
> Encil Mills. The road is rougher than ever. The
> fastest you can go is 20 m.p.h.. If you go faster you
> will bounce right thru the ceiling of the truck. The
> road is so bad you can't even read while you are
> moving as the book moves around too much. The
> truck rattles so much that you have to shout as loud
> as you can to talk to the driver who is sitting right
> next to you.

We apparently had some facilities and equipment available
to us for sports activities in our off-duty hours during my
early weeks in Korea, but I have no recollection of them. I
assume now that my lack of recall is because such facilities
were soon converted to housing quarters for the rapidly
expanding population that occurred shortly after I arrived
in camp. However, I know that the facilities must have
existed at one time because I mentioned them in my first
letter home from Camp Hillenmeyer:

> There is nothing to do or anywhere to go in our
> spare time, but I don't care. There is a nice day
> room in our Co. and plenty of athletic equipment.
> We'll amuse ourselves.

There was a great deal of camaraderie among the fellows
in each of the huts that I lived in. This was the case while I
was in the infantry and later during my assignment in the
engineer detachment. Most of our group entertainment
was informal and spontaneous.

We did find amusement in simple things. During winter months, a big snowfall was a great source of pleasure for us; it made us behave like unruly little children. Snow was rare where I grew up, so my first experience with horse-play in the snow shortly after my arrival in Korea was something to write home about:

> It started snowing nite before last so things outside were all white when we woke yesterday morning. It kept on snowing until about 2 in the afternoon. It snowed again last night and kept snowing all day. We had some physical training out in the snow, then class until noon. Being that today is Wednesday, we had the afternoon off.

> We had a big snowball fight a little while ago. Everybody got a good plastering. Somebody tackled me and we rassled [sic] out in the snow. Guys were rubbing each others faces with it. Boy, what a time. K & I Companies had the biggest fight I ever saw. About 200 guys were in it. Snowballs were coming down like rain.

Our "enemies" were also targets of our child-like snow play:

> The bugler sleeps in this hut and do we give him a bad time. The guys wake him up in the middle of the nite. He came out of the hut a couple of days ago right after it snowed and about 5 of us guys really snowballed him. What a laugh.

The battalion bugler's name was Garland P. Jones, and he came from Norfolk, Virginia. "Old Jones," as we called him, was a really nice guy, but we gave him a hard time just because he woke us up every morning. Whenever we had snowball fights, poor Old Jones got peppered mercilessly. He really gave us a great laugh one time when, after free beer night at the service club, he played mess call instead of taps.

During my second winter, the snow also provided us with other less harassing sports:

> It has been snowing quite a bit around here lately, but it isn't too cold. The temperature has been down to zero in the mornings, but by noon it's up to 10 or 15 degrees.

> I've been trying to learn how to ski, but so far I've done most of it on my hind end. You must be wondering where the ski equipment came from. It is army ski troop equipment. We also have a tobogan [sic]. We really have fun coming down hills with it as we tip over most of the time.

On cold winter evenings, the stove was the center of our social life:

> Although there is nothing to do around here, it seems like I'm always busy — mostly talking. We sit around the stove every nite and shoot the bull. I always hate to leave the conference, so that's why I write so few letters other than those I write home.

> The electric service around here is unpredictable. The lights go out without warning every once in a

while. When that happens we all gather around
the stove and sing songs. It is a lot of fun even if it
doesn't sound very good. We are like one big happy
family in this hut. If there is no entertainment, we
entertain ourselves.

Early in my tour in Korea, I wrote home often about one of
the fellows who brought a lot of fun and lightheartedness
into our lives:

There is a guy in our hut from Jersey City. His name
is Carmine Prinzo. Is he a character. He talks like a
dead-end kid, looks like Sad Sack, and is always
making a lot of noise. He's our main source of entertainment around here. Right now Prinzo is en-
tertaining the barracks — as usual. This time he is
singing Italian songs. Is he a riot.

During the warmer months, a few of us would take long
walks exploring the surrounding countryside. We often
went to the beach to walk, and talk, and sometimes rest:

Last Sunday a couple of us went out and laid on
the beach and read all afternoon, 'what a life.'

Occasionally, a group of us would organize an outdoor
game or perhaps just toss a football around:

Yesterday was Army Day so we had another day
off. Nothing much went on — we laid around the
barracks all day. After chow we played a little football and had a pretty good time.

My mother contributed often to our group entertainment:

> One of your letters contained that puzzle you sent
> and right now it's causing old Kennedy to get gray
> hair. It is first class entertainment around here. You
> say you couldn't figure it out. I couldn't at first
> either and thought you might have sent some odd
> pieces of cardboard as a joke on me. I kept work-
> ing on it and finally got it. I'll draw a solution for
> you [the accompanying drawing is a T, put together
> from four odd-shaped pieces]. Some other guys are
> playing with it now.

I remember well another source of fun my mother sent me.
It was a liquid plastic material that could be blown up into
a balloon when a small glob of it was placed on the end of
a straw. I wrote a letter of thanks:

> I received that package with the plastic balloon juice
> in it. We had a good time while it lasted. Every-
> body wanted to blow one up but there wasn't
> enough to go around. Anyway we still enjoyed it
> very much.

My letter encouraged my mother to send more:

> I just received another package the other day with
> cookies and fruit juice in it. It also had some more
> tubes of plastic balloons. The guys are beginning
> to wonder if my mother knows how old I am. Any-
> way, they were all blowing balloons the other day
> and enjoying it — so they can't say too much.

It would be more appropriate to call some of our group activities mischief rather than entertainment, but we viewed it as the latter and enjoyed it as such. Bed tipping was one such activity that took place with great regularity:

> The lights were out last Fri. nite and we were all in bed talking and not knowing what to do. Suddenly, some wise guy starts tipping beds over. Well, one guy won't stand for being tipped without revenge so you can imagine what a commotion there was. I got tipped once myself and don't think I didn't dump somebody else. Things like that go on and on. It's never peaceful around here.

> We have a lot of fun in the morning. After the C.Q. [Charge of Quarters] wakes us up we lie there half asleep and threaten to dump each other out of bed.

Episodes of bed tipping and other horseplay were interspersed with periods of calm:

> Things are quiet in the barracks lately. Not much noise, not much horsing around. The last commotion we had was when some guys were throwing dirty sox at each other 2 nites ago.

Any event that could give rise to some practical joke was never ignored:

> There is a fellow in the hut from Wisconsin named Zuberbuehler. His folks own a cheese factory. He got a package from home last nite with a great big

cheese in it. It was real good cheese, but did it stink! It stunk worse than limburger. The guys were threatening to bury the cheese and make him sleep outside.

One guy was asleep so another kid held a piece of this cheese under his nose. In about 2 seconds the guy was awake and cussing the cheese. That stuff really caused an uproar.

The saga of the stinking cheese continued in a letter dated two days later:

I guess you remember that stinking cheese I mentioned in the letter before this. This guy that owned the cheese kept it under his bed until yesterday afternoon. He was gone then so we put it in his bed. It stayed there until he found it after chow when he sat on his bed. Did he blow a fuse and did we laugh. He tried to blame it on somebody and we would all swear with straight faces that the accused was innocent.

The stink hit a new high today when some wise guy put a piece of that cheese on the stove. Ohhh...what a stink. It just about knocks you over when you come in the door. I wonder if we have seen the end of that cheese yet.

I cannot recall that we saw, or rather smelled, any more of that cheese. It obviously had a finite life and the last bit of it must finally have been consumed.

Structured recreational activities were almost nonexistent
during the time I was at Camp Hillenmeyer. The Red Cross
did try to organize some craft or hobby groups, such as the
photography class that I elected, but few materialized due
to lack of participants.

The Red Cross also arranged an occasional sight-seeing tour
or outing. These attracted more interest than the craft
classes and were more successful, weather permitting. A
sight-seeing tour to a silver smelter that I was most interested in was canceled because of rain. The only other such
outing that I recall was a boat trip on the Yellow Sea the
Sunday before Labor Day:

> I went on a boat trip on the Yellow Sea yesterday
> and had a pretty good time lying around and swim-
> ming. The Red Cross sponsored the trip for any
> G.I.s that wanted to go.
>
> We left camp about ten AM in two 1 1/2-ton trucks
> for the Kunsan docks. It took 40 minutes to cover
> the 9 miles to the docks. What a road. It's all bumps.
>
> The boat was a Japanese tugboat that was in very
> good condition. It was powered by a 3-cylinder
> Diesel engine that really shone. Those Koreans
> were constantly shining that engine. They could
> really crawl around that engine.
>
> The boat went out into the Yellow Sea a couple of
> miles and anchored. We went swimming off the
> boat in our underwear. Some of the guys even went
> in with their suntan pants on. The water was warm

and not very clear. I don't know how deep it was as I couldn't touch bottom. We swam for a couple of hours, ate sandwiches and doughnuts, then pulled up anchor and headed back to Kunsan. Got back to camp tired, dusty, and in one piece.

The USO put on two shows at Camp Hillenmeyer during 1947. The first was just before Memorial Day in May and the second was in early August on opening night of the new theater. Apparently there were no celebrities in either show. If there had been, I would have mentioned them in letters home. The show in May was memorable for another reason:

> I went to a USO show the other nite. It was pretty good. There was one act that had to have a hole cut in the ceiling so it would fit. The act was a guy that stood on his head on a chair that was balanced on a horizontal bar. When the guy got balanced up there, all you could see were his hands. The rest of him stuck up thru the ceiling.
>
> There also was a juggling act that wasn't bad.

The only other diversions available on a regular basis were provided by the movie theater and the service club. I seldom went to the theater prior to the opening of the new theater in August. The original theater, in an old Japanese barracks, was very uncomfortable, with hard benches and a small screen. The pictures that were shown were four to five years old and in such poor condition that it was a rare occasion if the film did not break at least once during the showing.

After the USO event on opening night of the new theater, I became a regular, but obviously not a happy, moviegoer:

> Movies are now being shown in the new theater. So far, the admission is still free. I guess one of these days they will start charging us 20¢.

> In a little while I'll put on my suntans and take a walk up to the service club to have a coke. Then, about 8 PM, 3 or 4 of us will go to the movies. That's all there is to do here and that is what I do just about every nite. The only thing different about each day is the picture at the show. Last night we saw another lousy picture. Maybe someday they'll get a good picture over here.

A recurring theme in my letters home during my entire stay at Camp Hillenmeyer was the subject of drinking. I did not drink while in the army, primarily because I disliked the taste of beer. However, I did have a strong distaste for drunkenness because of childhood memories of drunkards in our neighborhood who abused their families while under the influence, but I had no objection to moderate consumption of alcohol. In fact, wine was considered a food in the Italian culture in which I was raised.

I was not alone in being a nondrinker. The fellows I associated with most in off-duty hours drank very seldom or not at all. I wrote home about one of these friends when he was due to return to the States:

> One of the fellows who sleeps in this hut is leaving in a few days and I'm sure he will stop by to see

you if he lands in San Francisco. The bus passes through Santa Rosa on the way to Oregon where he's from. His name is Lloyd Wing (not Chinese, as the name implies) and he's my age. He is a swell guy. He used to be in the Merchant Marine, but he isn't a typical mariner. He doesn't drink or smoke.

Unfortunately, my folks never got to meet Wing. I had a letter from him in early May saying that he had landed in Seattle rather than San Francisco and, thus, did not pass through Santa Rosa on the way home.

My first lengthy report of drinking in camp was in a letter dated March 17, about two months after my arrival:

I told you in a previous letter that our money was taken away from us because of some sort of black market worry. After a week with no money at all in camp, the fellows got kind of thirsty. We got different money yesterday. It's in $ and¢ and it's red.

Now to get back to the point of the fellows being thirsty. This situation of no liquor for a week while there was no money threw the whole camp in an uproar when there was money again. There were two guys from our hut that had to be dragged from the club. They were dead drunk. Five other guys were happy. They threw the whole barracks into an uproar. It's a wonder the buildings stand up under the beating they take.

The cooks were all drunk and the mess sergeant got so drunk he went crazy. They took him to Seoul this morning. There was an armed guard over him all nite because they were afraid he'd kill somebody. He threatened to kill one of the cooks and the cook flattened him. He walked into the latrine and heard a kid that was sitting there say the food was lousy so he [mess sgt.] hauls off and socks the kid in the jaw and says, 'I'll show you if the food is good.'

Nobody liked him anyway as he used to give the KPs a bad time. One time he kept the KPs for 23 hours GI-ing the floors and everything. I could tell by the way he talked that he was crazy anyway.

Rumor had it that the mess sergeant was sent to the Pong Song Prison, an army facility in South Korea where enlisted men who contracted venereal diseases were sent for a period up to six months for both treatment and punishment.

Our replacement mess sergeant lacked a violent temper but had a similar drinking problem:

We have a new mess sergeant and he is worse than the old one. He's been here 3 days and I haven't seen him sober yet. This place is getting to be a drunkard's paradise. You'd be surprised at how many guys get plastered around here, not every week but about every other nite. None of the guys have the "shakes" yet, but it won't be long.

On several occasions, our Company gave us a party, with ample supplies of beer and cokes. At one party that was held in the mess hall we also had all the hot dogs we could eat. During the warm summer months the parties were held on the beach. Regardless of location, the parties always ended with some of the participants going to excess:

> We had a beer party at the beach this afternoon. Boy, what a bunch of drunks. What a place. The main entertainment is drinking. It's a good thing there were trucks around to haul the guys back.

The ingenuity and stamina of some of the heavy drinkers amazed me. While I was in G Company during the summer of 1947, I wrote:

> Boy, is there a bunch of rugged guys in the hut I am sleeping in now. They mix up 'footlocker cocktails' and drink them. Shaving lotion, hair tonic, shoe polish, and anything with alcohol in it they'll drink. I've heard about such things, but didn't think they actually happened. The funny part of it is they don't even wake up with a hangover.

This group also carved initials on each other with sharpened knives and bayonets during their drinking bouts. They would wander around the barracks with blood all over their arms and chests. We thought they were crazy — literally.

The excessive drinking on the part of the troops at Camp Hillenmeyer was depressing to me not for any moral reasons, as I have said, but rather because it seemed like such waste of youthful talent and an insult to young healthy bodies. It did not bother me so much that older men and officers drank to excess, but I was concerned for other fellows my own age:

It's a shame that there is no restriction on the sale of liquor to minors. A lot of kids 18 or less get so drunk they have to be carried back to their barracks.

I was even more angry at the army for not providing some wholesome choices for the enlisted men. I was too young to know what should be done, nevertheless I knew the way it was, was wrong:

It's Sat. nite. Most of the guys are out getting drunk, as usual. It's too bad there isn't some other entertainment to keep the guys occupied so they wouldn't drink so much. Same old thing every nite; eat, put on some suntans, and go to the I.P. (Service Club). Some of the guys are getting red faces like regular old soaks.

Gambling was another common pastime. However, that did not bother me as much as the drinking. In fact it kept some fellows sober for lack of funds:

We got paid this afternoon and already the guys are gambling. There is a big crap game going on in the back of the hut. It seems the only thing guys do with money around here is gamble. Last month one guy lost $650 in one roll.

Poker was another popular game of chance:

We got paid the other nite and a lot of the guys are already broke. I don't see how they do it. Month after month they go busted, yet they keep on playing poker.

I finally got a money order for last month's pay. It's only $60 because I loaned out $25 to my broke buddies. What guys. They get paid and the next day they are broke from playing poker. I'll send you the extra $25 next payday. The guys are always good for it.

In November 1947, I was eligible for a military sponsored Rest and Recreation (R&R) furlough. I signed up for a trip to the port city of Shanghai. A troop ship would take about a thousand soldiers to Shanghai where we would spend three days sight-seeing in and around the city. We would live aboard the troop ship while in China.

I was very excited about the prospect of visiting the Chinese mainland and seeing the ancient city of Shanghai. However, the trip was canceled because the Nationalist government of Chiang Kai-shek was losing control of the country and retreating southward toward Shanghai. The army was worried that Chinese Nationalist control of the countryside around Shanghai might collapse. Such an eventuality would make our trip unsafe and put us in too much danger.

From time to time, a few soldiers were selected to take R&R trips to special resorts operated by the U.S. Army in Japan, but I decided not even to request one. The reason, I told myself, was that I did not want to spend my hard-earned money on a trip to a place where women and low-cost liquor were the main attraction. I was saving every penny I could for my schooling. I felt a trip to Shanghai, on the other hand, would have been money well spent because it was old Orient, unaffected by American troops.

Looking back, I believe the real reason I did not want to go to Japan was a subliminal fear that I could not face the reality of having to return to Korea and Camp Hillenmeyer. All of the fellows from camp who had gone to Japan came back clean and rested. They were well-groomed, with neat haircuts and fresh clothes. They told of the good food and pleasant accommodations they had. I had gotten used to being cold, and hungry, and grubby. I did not want to leave my uncomfortable situation only to have to return to it.

My substitute for a visit to Shanghai was a 3-day pass to Seoul, the capitol of South Korea, two days of which were spent on the train. I described the trip in a letter home on December 15:

> John Carrol and I left here on Saturday morning at 10 AM on the mail truck. It was cold as blank, but we had our parkas which kept us pretty warm. We made it to Iri by 11:30 without any casualties except a broken radiator hose on the truck.
>
> We caught the train at 2 PM. It was 9 hours late, it's supposed to come thru at 5 AM. [Because trains were always many hours late, we knew that by leaving camp at 10:00 AM we still had time to catch the 5:00 AM train.] The train had one G.I. coach on it, the rest of the cars were Korean. I'll try to describe the car we rode in. It was in surprisingly good shape. It had all its seats and windows. It was a Japanese sleeper, which is an exact copy of an American Pullman except that the berths are shorter. You have to curl up slightly to fit in one. The cars the Koreans were in had no windows,

some seats, and were overflowing with people. They were hanging out all over the place.

These Korean engines are really something. They don't have bells or lights. They go full blast and blow the whistle. Also they don't have much power. When they start upgrade they start slowing down. Slower and slower they go until they are barely moving. When they reach the top then they gain speed downhill till they are just about flying.

We arrived in Seoul about noon Sunday. It's a pretty big city, has streetcars and paved streets. The streets are crowded with ox carts, handcarts, 3-wheeled taxis, jeeps, miniature automobiles and horse drawn busses. It has some modern buildings and many wooden shacks. It looks like Chinatown in Santa Rosa used to, only worse.

There is a beautiful theater for the troops right in the main part of town, with a coffee shop underneath. A couple of blocks away is a 3-story PX with a snack bar underneath. The guys stationed around Seoul really have a good deal compared to the 63rd.

I ran into a couple of guys I knew during the day. We went to the movie in the afternoon, then roamed around to 8:30 PM when our train left. Arrived at Iri at 2 PM Monday and here I am.

After my brief visit to Seoul, I began thinking about leaving Korea and wondering when orders for my return trip home would come through. I also had time to reflect on my experiences of the past year. Happily, I would be leaving the army and the poor land that was Korea, but what was the future of the Korean people whom I had observed but not really seen very clearly?

CHAPTER FIFTEEN

KUNSAN
AND ITS PEOPLE

One of our first orders on arriving in Korea in January 1947, was not to fraternize or have any commerce with the Korean people. The army was very firm about this. We were told not to eat any food or drink any water outside of camp because it was considered unsafe by the military authorities. Kunsan, the only town nearby, was off limits for most of the time I was in Korea. We were not permitted to go off base except on official business. Only twice during my 14-month stay in Korea did I receive a pass to go to town. Even when we received passes, we could only visit certain areas; the rest of the town was off limits.

Kunsan is one of the five major cities in Chollabuk-Do Province, the other four are Chonju, Chongju, Iri, and Namwon. The Kum River flows westward through the large coastal lowland of Chollabuk-Do Province to the sea through Kunsan harbor. The province is slightly larger than 3000 square miles and, with the exception of a few hills, is the largest flat area in all of Korea. This topographical feature suits the province to agriculture and makes it the rice basket of South Korea.

Kunsan is a port city on the Yellow Sea, about 150 miles south of Seoul. In recent years, an outer harbor west of the old harbor has been created by dredging and new port facilities have been built. However, at the time I was in Korea, old Kunsan harbor was small and silted, with no good anchorage and a wide tidal range.

A difference of up to 40 feet between low and high tides made floating docks necessary. These docks were constructed in such a way that a ship could tie up to a barge-like float that would rise and fall with the tide. The float, in turn, was connected to the wharf by a hinged ramp over which freight and passengers could move between ship and shore.

In 1947, the port area of Kunsan was relatively small and only deep enough to accommodate shallow-draft ships. The port consisted of two or three floating docks, about a dozen single story concrete warehouses, and a small railroad yard. This yard was served by a branch railroad line that connected to the north-south main line at Iri, a small town about 30 miles inland to the east.

Kunsan's major landmark was a nonferrous smelter. It was built on the north shore of the harbor, opposite the town of Kunsan, which was on the south shore. Although the smelter was not operating in 1947, its tall concrete smokestack made it visible for miles around.

Kunsan's other landmark was a former Japanese air field, about nine miles south of the city on the shore of the Yellow Sea. It had been built many years before, during the period when Korea was occupied and controlled by the Japanese. This air base had a grass landing strip, which was common at the time, three large hangars, and wooden barracks that could accommodate about 500 military personnel. The base was taken over and occupied by the 63rd Infantry Regiment when the U.S. Army occupied the area in late 1945. Shortly after, the base was given the name Camp Hillenmeyer

Today, Kunsan is a major shipping center with a population of over 180,000. However, the Kunsan I knew in 1947 had a population of only 40,000 and was by no means a modern city. Most streets were unpaved and there were few sidewalks. Most of the buildings were single story wood and mud structures with thatched roofs. A few two and three story battered-looking concrete buildings with broken windows were located near the center of town. Interestingly, most of these concrete buildings had an art-deco architectural style that was popular in the United States in the 1930's.

The town had no sewage system. Householders dumped their sewage into large ceramic jars about ten gallons in size. These jars, known as honey buckets or honey jars, were stored outside the houses near the street. They were emptied weekly by horse-drawn honey carts. The honey carts delivered their loads to the surrounding countryside, where the human sewage was used as fertilizer for growing rice and vegetables.

My first trip to Kunsan occurred about two weeks after I arrived at Camp Hillenmeyer. In a letter dated January 25, 1947, I described the trip to my brother Bob:

> I went to Kunsan the other day. It wasn't on a pass, but a coal detail. When we got in town, which is about nine miles from camp, there wasn't any coal so we came right back.
>
> The road leading to town is dirt and extremely rough. The highest speed possible on this road is 20 MPH on the smooth stretches, which are few.
>
> Kunsan has one paved street and 5 or 6 modern buildings that have taken quite a beating. There were a few electric wires around. They were about 15 ft off the ground and strung all around with no set plan.
>
> All you see on the way to town and back are rice paddies and grass houses. There were a lot of locals walking on the road. They would scatter when the truck came along. They are scared of U.S. vehicles. Maybe it's because mufflers are unknown around here. All the trucks and jeeps sound like airplanes.

I received my first pass to Kunsan about a month later, on February 25:

> Now I'll describe the town. We enter Kunsan from the camp side thru a tunnel about 500 ft long. On the top of the hill that the tunnel goes thru is some

kind of a temple that overlooks the town. It is the prettiest part of the whole town.

The main street takes off from the tunnel and runs about 1/2 mile. The buildings are all one story wood and unpainted. The street is poorly paved so it is half mudd [sic].

The people walk on the street just like they do on the sidewalks as there are hardly any vehicles. There are no neon signs around or anything to make it look like the States.

The women wear real long skirts and most of them have packages which they carry very easily on their heads.

What I noticed most was the smell. The town just smells rotten; like a cow barn.

I went to the post office to buy a few Korean stamps. I thought you might like to see them. The post office is a small granite building with a dirty appearance. I think it's just there to sell stamps to GI's as I didn't see any mail in there.

Several months later I made another trip to Kunsan, this time on a work detail to repair some telephone wiring at L Company's quarters in the old monastery on the far side of Kunsan. This trip gave me the opportunity to see not only the monastery, but also more of downtown Kunsan. The monastery was very old and set on hill overlooking the countryside. It was in a very peaceful setting with a view of the harbor. L Company was stationed there because it was responsible for continuous guard duty in the port area of nearby Kunsan.

While on actual guard duty, soldiers from L Company stayed in a three-story concrete building on a main street in Kunsan. The building, called the KCC building, was one of the very few western-style buildings in Kunsan. KCC was said to stand for Kunsan Chamber of Commerce, but that did not seem logical to me. The building, from its size and construction, made me conclude that it must have been built by the Japanese for their own use.

Every piece of glass in the KCC building was broken out. The entryway had double swinging doors with their glass panels missing. It was an unusual sight to watch soldiers entering and leaving the building by just stepping through places in the door that had once been filled by glass panels, rather than by opening the doors.

Another notable feature of the building was that it had no latrines for the approximately 50 soldiers who stayed there between shifts during their 24-hour periods of guard duty. As a result, the alley in back of the building was, for all practical purposes, impassable.

In the cold winter months of early 1947, the KCC building was the equivalent of living outdoors in the bitter cold. The interior was bare concrete. Every window was broken out and there was no heating system. The only furnishings were cots with no blankets. Whenever I passed through there in my job of repairing telephone wires, I felt blessed that I did not have to spend days and nights in that place.

Despite our limited access to town, Koreans were no strangers to the camp. When I first arrived, Koreans were employed as houseboys and kitchen aides. Korean children would sneak into camp to sell trinkets to the soldiers. My first encounter with the little merchants happened during my first week in camp:

> I was out behind the hut a little while ago doing some business with some Korean kids. That's the only way we can buy Korean merchandise around here because nobody gets passes. We have to stay in the camp.

> I just traded 2 packs of cigarettes (13 cents or 60 yen) for the silk handkerchief you found enclosed. They don't have much variety, but little by little I'll accumulate some souvenirs. I will also send home some yen in another letter. It is easy to get for cigarettes. The kids run around with pockets of yen trying to buy stuff off of us.

We saw many Korean people not only in camp but also along the roads between the camp and Kunsan. I had concluded that the fright the Koreans displayed when they saw or heard us approaching was due to the noise our trucks made. It was not long before I realized my reasoning was naive. It soon became obvious that the Koreans were as afraid of the soldiers as they were of their vehicles:

> A lot of locals use the road between here and Kunsan and do they take a beating from the vehicle drivers. They try to see how close they can

come to the Koreans and their ox-carts — like the other day. I wasn't in the jeep that did it, but a fellow from the hut was. There is a lake by the side of the road, what I mean is the road runs on a dike that holds in the lake. The edge of the road drops about 7 ft directly into the water. Anyway, this jeep came up right next to a man that was riding a bicycle by the edge of the lake. When the jeep got alongside the bicycle, one of the guys gave the Korean a big push and down he went, bicycle and all, into that cold water. That's an example of how the locals get treated along the roads.

My mother was not pleased that her son was associated with people who behaved in such a manner. She worried about its effect on my safety, and questioned me further. In retrospect, I am sure my response did not help allay her fears:

Don't worry about the Koreans being unfriendly. They don't show it, but I don't think they like us too much because the guys give them a bad time when they can. For example, they aren't safe on the roads where there are U.S. vehicles because the guys see how close they can come to the Koreans walking along. They drive by and reach out and steal the Koreans' hats right off their heads.

Are they friendly? It's hard to say. They have been dominated by the Japanese for so long that they don't know themselves. I think it depends on who is in power. They say they liked the Japanese and they say they like us. It's hard to figure out.

One type of mistreatment of the local people that was fairly common during my first winter in Korea was the Shanghaiing of Korean men for work details. One such event that is still vivid in my mind occurred when I was assigned with three or four other GI's to a work detail supervised by a noncommissioned officer, a sergeant, if I remember correctly. He picked us up in a six-by-six truck and told us we were going to Kunsan to load the truck with sacks of cement. On the way, the sergeant told the driver to stop next to four or five Korean men who were walking along the side of the road.

With a menacing shout, the sergeant motioned the men to get in the back of the truck. They objected, but reluctantly got in the back with us when the sergeant brandished a pistol. The truck then drove to a warehouse in Kunsan and backed up to the loading dock. The sergeant jumped out and shouted to us, "Don't let those Gooks get out of the truck." Then he made clear to the Koreans, by motions and pigeon English, that the price of their freedom was to load the truck with sacks of cement from the warehouse. With much protesting, they loaded the truck, while those of us who were supposed to do the work sat and watched.

As I relaxed while the Koreans worked, many thoughts went through my mind. I was disturbed by the Shanghaiing, even though I knew it was beyond my control, but strangely, I was even more uncomfortable about an aspect of the situation that most people would probably consider a far more trivial matter. The cement sacks were leaky and dusty so that, in the process of loading, the Koreans became covered from head to foot in cement dust. On seeing this, I wondered about how these men were going to clean themselves. We had not had easy access to showers or clean clothes for several months. Being dirty all of the time had become noticeably unpleasant. While watching these Koreans load cement it occurred to me that they probably had similar problems with bathing, which were being worsened by the cement dust. I thought how wrong it was to make people work against their will, but how much worse it was to force them to get dirty when there was no easy way for them to get clean.

When the trucks were loaded, the sergeant immediately released the Koreans. This was in front of a warehouse on a very cold day in the seaport area of Kunsan. Because we had picked the men up on a road about five or six miles away, one of us asked the sergeant, "How are these poor bastards going to get home?" His terse response was, "They'll figure it out." With that we drove away, leaving the Koreans standing on a cold, empty street.

Most of the acts of malevolence by soldiers against the Korean men occurred during my first winter in Korea. It seemed that such episodes were committed primarily by soldiers who had arrived in Korea before my group got there. As these soldiers went home, harsh treatment of Korean individuals became less frequent and eventually almost nonexistent.

I often wondered, even many years after I left Korea, why a few soldiers treated the local Korean people so badly. American soldiers are not basically cruel men. During World War II they were trained to kill the enemy, but they did not engage in acts of brutality and torture, as some barbaric armies do against their prisoners and even against civilian men, women, and children. Interestingly, our soldiers were not unkind to Korean women and children. In fact, quite the opposite; the children, especially, stole the hearts of our servicemen.

Many years later I read that General Hodge, Commander of the U.S. Forces in Korea at the time, was very disturbed by the attitudes of the GI's toward the Korean people. He instituted a courtesy drive to control disrespectful acts such as whistling at Korean girls, practical jokes on Korean men, and the deliberate running of vehicles through the omnipresent muddy spots in order to splash water and mud on Korean people. General Hodge apparently felt that the problems were due to the quality of the officers assigned to Korean duty and the immaturity of teenage GI's (Smith, page 34).

Interestingly, I have no recollection of any officer ever talking to us about respecting the dignity of the Korean people and treating them kindly.

In retrospect, perhaps the roots of such behavior can be traced, at least in part, to some of the American blunders in the initial stages of the occupation. A brief history of the American occupation of Korea, presented in Chapter Eighteen, gives little reason to expect that there could have been amicable relations between our servicemen and the Korean people. Cruel or harsh acts by American soldiers against Korean people, deplorable as they were, seemed no worse than those committed by some Koreans themselves:

A couple of Koreans got in a fight the other day while they were shoveling some dirt. They don't

believe in fighting fair at all. In the fight I am talking about now, a big guy was hitting a little kid,
who was down, with a shovel. If I hadn't of come
along and stopped the fight, I know the kid would
have gotten killed. There were about ten Koreans
standing around watching but not one of them even
made an attempt to stop it.

Young men or boys seemed the most common victims. I
came to the conclusion that every culture must have its
bullies:

> I've seen a Korean cop kick a little kid right in the
> stomach so hard that the kid keeled over.

Apparently cruelty among Koreans was more common than
I realized. In a discussion of the cruel treatment of their
captives by the North Koreans, the late Marguerite Higgins
wrote as follows:

> This is not surprising, as both North and South
> Koreans are notorious for their cruelty (Higgins,
> page 208).

Except for the children who crept into camp to sell things,
I had little direct contact with individual Koreans until
about six months after my arrival. However, it only took a
few weeks to begin to really appreciate the privations of
the people. On February 8, after my first garbage detail I
wrote:

> The people in the U.S. don't realize how lucky they
> are. The other day I had the good (hah) fortune of

being on a garbage detail for about $^1/_2$ hr. We picked up about 5 garbage cans of slop at the mess hall and took them to the dump. When we got about $^1/_4$ of a mile from the dump, Koreans started coming toward us from all directions. We stopped at the dump and they swarmed all around waiting for us to dump the cans.

They [garbage cans] were pretty heavy so we just pushed can and all over the end of the trailer. The garbage hit and made a great big splash that just about drowned a few people nearby. As soon as the garbage hit the ground they went after it on their hands and knees with their bare hands. Some of them had [small] cans which they filled with stuff they picked out of the garbage.

The Koreans who worked in camp also kept an eye out for anything we discarded:

The Koreans pick up all the used cans we throw away and take them to town and make all kinds of buckets, pans and other tin ware. They are really artists at that work.

The incredible contrast between poverty in the United States and poverty in other less developed parts of the world, such as Korea, was revealed to me many times while I was overseas, but never more sadly than on Easter day, April 6, 1947. The weather was beautiful, cool and clear, with the sun shining brightly. It was a happy day until I decided to take a walk that afternoon up to the top of Blacktop Mountain, once used as a fortification by the Japanese:

It has caves and foxholes all over it. The caves were dug out of the rock and only about 20 ft long. Some of the larger caves had Koreans living in them. The people living in the caves had by far the lowest standard of living I've seen yet.

I feel sorry for these poor people, they really have a hard life. The people living in the U.S. don't know how lucky they are.

Our observations of the difficulties and hardships suffered by the Korean poor, as limited as they were, made me realize how fortunate I was:

You won't see me complaining anymore when I get back to the good old U.S. No matter how bad off I am in the States, I'll be living like a god compared to these Koreans. I can't describe in writing how things are here. You'll have to wait until I get home.

The dietary pattern and agricultural practices of the Koreans held a great fascination for me, perhaps because I was raised in a farming community and had picked a lot of fruit and hops as a youngster. I had seen a few vegetables used by the Koreans that were unfamiliar to me. I thought it would be interesting to get some seeds to send to my parents for their vegetable garden. I wrote home about my idea, but never had success in obtaining seeds:

I'll try to find some local vegetable seeds besides rice. I haven't seen much of anything here except rice and grass. The main diet of these people is rice and fish so I doubt if I find anything.

The scarcity of livestock impressed me:

> The Koreans around here don't have any cows as
> far as I know. They have a few chickens that run
> around loose. They live mostly on rice. The whole
> country around here is covered with rice paddies.

Fish apparently was an important part of the Korean diet.
Local people fished in the Yellow Sea. The beach near Camp
Hillenmeyer was a long mud flat at low tide. The beach
was so shallow that at low tide you could not see the water
when standing on the shoreline. On a few occasions, we
tried to walk out to the water's edge when the tide was
low, but we gave it up as an impossibility; we would sink
down to our knees in mud. Yet we often saw Koreans walking out on top of the mud at low tide to fish in the distant
water. How they did it we did not know, but we decided
they must have known of narrow pathways of solid ground
in the mud.

Often, when we visited the beach just after high tide, we
saw little Korean children scampering around on the sand,
laughing and giggling. After the tide had peaked, the beach
would be dotted with many tiny crabs scooting around on
the sand, apparently trying to return to the water after being beached by the receding tide. They were sand crabs,
about the size of a half dollar. The children would run after the tiny crabs, snatch them up, hurriedly wipe them on
their clothing to clean away the sand, and then pop them
live into their mouths. They ate the little crabs with obvious gusto, and then ran after more. We would watch in
amazement, wondering what it must feel like to chew and
swallow a live, wriggling little creature.

In late October, the rice crop was ready for harvest. On a trip to Kunsan during the harvest season I had the opportunity to see some of the activity:

> The Koreans were harvesting their rice when we went by. They use primitive methods. They use sickles to cut it with and ox carts to haul it to town. The way they get the rice off the stalk is by putting it on a big mat and beating it with sticks.

We never received any official news or information about any troubles or difficulties relating to the Koreans in camp. As a result, when anything out of the ordinary happened it was the subject of much rumor and speculation. One such event was the shooting of two Koreans the night of March 17-18, 1947. Their bodies were dragged into camp, deposited near I Company, and left on view for most of the day. I am sure that my mother was not comforted by my account of the event:

> We had a little action around here yesterday. Two Koreans got shot. There were about 7 of them stealing clothes around here for about a week. They used to come in on a boat and come ashore at the beach which is about $1/2$ mile from here. They would come in at nite, sneak in the tents, and take duffel bags of clothes back to the boats and get away.
>
> Nobody saw who was taking the stuff until a Korean stole 2 blankets off a guy who was asleep. He woke up just in time to see the Koreans going out of the tent. They got away, though, because he

couldn't wake up the other guys in the tent fast enough.

The next night a squad of men went out to the beach about 10 PM and waited for them. They had 1 BAR and the rest M-1's. About midnite, the Koreans came ashore. The Americans had it all planned ahead, and let the Koreans go into the tents again and take more to make sure they were getting the right ones. When the Koreans tried to get back to their boat, the squad opened up and killed two of them. The BAR got jammed or they would have got all seven. [BAR stands for Browning Automatic Rifle, a light 30-caliber machine gun that looks like an oversized rifle]

By the end of March all Korean service workers were gone from the camp. Rightly or wrongly, we did not associate their disappearance with the shooting. Instead we blamed it on resentments within the camp and a feeling that the Korean staff were being better fed than we were.

The ban on Korean workers in the living and administration areas of the camp was lifted a number of months later. One of the few services brought back to camp was a barber shop:

I got a haircut last nite in the local barber shop. The barbers are Korean. They are getting so they can do a pretty good job for 20 cents. Besides giving a haircut, they give a massage on your shoulders, neck & head. Slightly different from an American job.

In early April we heard rumors that the army was going to intensify its efforts to eliminate the black market. We were issued orders that we were not to give anything made in the United States to the Koreans. It was stressed that such transactions were illegal. We did not understand what all the fuss was about. The only things we could trade or sell were cigarettes, candy, and soap, and they were all rationed. The more affluent Koreans would have given just about anything for our clothing, other equipment, or food, but we had such short supply of those items for ourselves that we had none to spare.

The Koreans had no use for our invasion money and we had no use for their yen, except to buy trinkets, silk goods, and food. Cigarettes were useful to obtain services such as laundry and haircuts. Within a few months I had obtained all the souvenirs I wanted. Thus, since I did not smoke, I stopped taking my ration of cigarettes.

We suspected that if a black market were operating, it was on a much higher level than that of lowly privates. We were also quite sure that there was a great deal of stealing, small scale and large, by both Koreans and Americans. For the most part, stealing by Americans was prompted by avarice, whereas stealing by Koreans was motivated by poverty.

We knew from letters from home that many parcel post packages sent to us were never received. We knew too that we never received much of the food, clothing, and other supplies that the army claimed they shipped to us. The supply route between Inch'on and Camp Hillenmeyer was a very leaky one. Eventually, in order to ensure safe deliv-

ery of supplies, armed soldiers had to ride the trains to protect them against hungry Koreans. The GI's who served as
train guards had an extremely uncomfortable and dangerous mission.

In my job with the Post Engineers I came into close contact
with many of the Korean men and boys who worked for
us. For the most part, except for carpenters and a few contractors, the people we hired were unskilled laborers. My
job was to explain and supervise the work. We were for-
bidden to fraternize with the Korean people, but we could
not help becoming fairly well acquainted with some of them
during working hours.

Part of the daily routine was to meet with Korean contractors and workers out at the job sites to review plans and
check on progress. For these meetings, the Koreans never
sought a pile of lumber or a box to sit on. Instead they
always squatted in a small circle. Squatting was common
in Korea for resting, working, and conversing. In fact, chairs
and the sitting posture were not common sights in Korea.
I had no choice but to squat also, or be the odd person either standing or kneeling at job site meetings.

After several weeks, during which my body must have
adapted to the squatting position, I found it a comfortable
resting position. I also learned in subsequent years that
squatting relaxes back muscles and has the effect of reduc-
ing back pains.

Also in later years, I wondered about the small circle of
squatters that formed spontaneously at those meetings.
Was this based on oriental wisdom? Did they know some-

thing that we did not know? Today, American group psychologists will tell you that the common configurations used for meetings in the western world, where the boss either stands in front of the group or sits at the head of the table, are not very effective, because they stifle two-way communications between the boss and the group. In such a setting, the boss appears as an authority figure and the group listens, but tends not to provide useful feedback.

The simple circle, on the other hand, particularly with everyone squatting on the ground, exerts a powerful leveling effect. The circle contains no position of authority; everyone occupies a position of equal status. In addition, according to today's experts, the circle is the best configuration for constructive two-way communication.

Korean laborers used a very interesting device called a chigeh (pronounced chi ge') to carry all sorts of heavy loads. It was a simple device, yet the most ingeniously designed backpack I have ever seen. It must have been perfected by hundreds of years of use in the ancient past, perhaps well before the wheel was known to the Korean people.

I had often wondered why there were no wheelbarrows in Korea while I was there. Perhaps it was because wheelbarrows could not be made out of tree branches and straw as were chigehs, but it was more likely that the chigeh worked better than the wheelbarrow in Korea where the countryside was mountainous and there was a lot of mud and not much pavement.

The chigeh could be described as an open-topped capital A, or perhaps a wide-bottomed capital H. It was built from two fairly straight tree limbs, about one to one-and-a-half inches in diameter and about five feet long. These two limbs made the two sides of the A. The two sides were connected at the crossbar of the A by a square frame about one foot on a side. This frame was padded with straw, and was designed to fit against the wearer's back like the padding on our modern backpacks. A woven straw strap that fit over the shoulder was fastened to each leg of the A, with one attachment a little above the padded frame and a second about one foot below the padded frame.

A piece of strong wood, or peg, a little more than a foot long was inserted at an upward angle into a hole drilled in the back of each leg of the A, just below the padded frame. These two pegs pointed directly backward and sloped upward forming the base for placing loads on the chigeh. Sacks of cement, for example, were carried by setting them on a short board placed against the A on top of the pegs.

In many cases, a branch of the tree limb used for the leg of an A served as the peg. When a tree limb, suitable for the leg of a chigeh, could be found that had a branch at the appropriate place, there was no need to drill a hole for inserting a peg.

The legs of the chigeh were cut so that the bottom ends of the A were about one foot above the ground when the wearer was standing. The upper ends extended about head high or sometimes higher. When using a chigeh, the wearer carried a walking stick about five feet long that was forked at the top. The stick made it easier to walk with a loaded chigeh, but it also had another important use. It also made it easy to stop and rest by serving as the third leg of a tripod, permitting the chigeh to stand alone. To accomplish this, the wearer simply squatted by bending at the knees until the legs of the A touched the ground. Then he leaned forward and placed the fork of the walking stick in a notch at the top center of the back pad, on the wearer's side. In this way, the third leg of a tripod was formed and the load would stand by itself.

A free-standing, loaded chigeh could be picked up easily by bending the knees slightly and slipping into the straps while removing the stick. This also made lifting the load much easier because the wearer could bend forward and use strong leg muscles to raise the load.

Chigehs were essential tools for the Korean method of mixing cement. I did not describe chigehs in letters home, but I did mention my appreciation of the Korean laborers in the way they did the job:

> They mix all their cement by hand. Two Koreans can mix cement faster than 20 GI's. They have a certain system in which every movement counts. They work together just like a machine. It's really interesting to watch.

> You should have 4 or 5 Koreans to do the cement work for that new cabin you are building. For a pack of cigarettes apiece they will work from dawn to sunset.

The method used for mixing concrete in Korea in 1947 was fast, effective, and ingenious, but very different from what I had seen at home. In the 1940's, in America, there were

no ready-mix trucks that delivered concrete ready for pour-
ing directly into forms, as there are today, but there were
gasoline-powered machines that mixed concrete at the job
site. Freshly mixed concrete was moved by wheelbarrows
and dumped into the forms.

In the Korean method of those days, a sheet of steel plate,
four feet wide and eight feet long, was set up with one of
the long edges overlapping the edge of a concrete form. A
temporary platform was constructed alongside the form,
if necessary, to support the steel plate.

Mixing was done on the steel plate by six shovelers, three
working from each side of the two long edges of the sheet.
If needed, planks were placed on the form for the shovelers to stand on. They used special short-handle shovels
with rectangular, flat blades about six inches wide and eight
inches long. Measured amounts of sand, gravel, cement,
and water were delivered by other workers who carried
these materials to the steel plate.

Chigehs were used to transport the necessary materials.
For the concrete mixing job, an open-ended straw basket
(formed like a taco shell) was placed on a board that sat on
the pegs of the chigeh. The basket was loaded with sand
or gravel, while the chigeh was in the tripod position, by
workers using shovels. When loaded, the chigeh was
picked up by its carrier and moved to the job.

The whole operation was governed by a chant that began
with the rattling of shovels on the steel plate. Cement sacks
were dumped from chigehs onto the steel plate. The sacks
were broken open with shovels and emptied onto the plate.

The pace of the chant changed then from a slow drone to a sprightly beat. Four or five carriers began moving in sequence with their chigehs, bringing sand and gravel at the times they were needed. As they walked by, the carriers leaned sideways, spilling their loads onto the steel plate as the shovelers, working in unison and chanting, repeatedly slid their shovels toward the center of the pile, twisted the shovels and flipped the mixture.

When the dry materials were sufficiently mixed, the chant changed again and workers carrying long poles over their shoulders, with water buckets swinging on each end of their poles, brought water for the mixing process.

In preparation for the addition of water, a well was made in the center of the dry mix — "Just like making pasta," I thought at the time. Water was poured from the buckets into the well and mixed in so quickly and rhythmically that not a drop of water rolled off the steel sheet. Quickly the batch changed to fresh, wet concrete and, again, the chant changed, telling the shovelers to immediately push the batch off the steel plate directly into the form.

When the steel plate had been scraped clean, the rattling of shovels on the steel plate and the chanting began again for mixing of the next batch of cement. When a section of the form was filled, the steel plate was moved ahead and the whole ritual repeated until the entire form was filled. Breaks in the regular work, such as lunch or quitting time, were signaled with a special chant that brought extra water carriers and started a sequence that thoroughly washed the steel plate clean.

One very interesting characteristic of Korean laborers was that, once given an order by a GI, they would continue doing what they were told even though logic would tell them to stop. Why, I never knew, but it certainly was not stupidity:

> All I did yesterday was sit in a truck and talk to the driver while the Korean crew loaded it. I had to tell them when to stop shoveling when the truck was full. If you don't tell them to stop they will bury the truck. After the truck was loaded we drove a little way and then I'd tell the Koreans to unload it. I didn't have to tell them to stop when the truck was empty.

The need for constant supervision was one of the frustrations and drawbacks with some Korean crews. I decided that much of it was due to their lack of knowledge of how to build western-style structures. Every day I spent an hour or two making the rounds of the various jobs in progress to make sure that no mistakes were made.

Despite their willingness and stamina, almost every day brought a surprise — a new interpretation of the construction plans. Some of the surprises made me chuckle:

> The Koreans can hammer and saw OK, but that's all. They don't know how to put a building up. I'll tell you what happened today. I walked into a day room the Koreans are building and they had all the moldings nailed up to the studs. They were figuring on putting up the sheeting and wallboard after

the molding. The same kind of thing happens all the time. The Koreans spend half their time tearing down their mistakes.

In the early summer, the responsibility for supervising their own construction jobs was given to Korean contractors:

> You remember the ditch I was working on? Well, the Koreans took a contract on it for 640,000 yen. I won't have to worry about that anymore.

> The Koreans are also building a new theater for us. Every once in a while I go over and check on them to see if they are doing things right. You ought to see those Korean contractors when I come around. They put on a big smile and treat me like I was a big shot. You ought to see me checking up around and looking at plans like I really knew what was going on. Again, as I say, 'What a laugh.'

I still remember well my contacts with one of the Korean contractors. I am not sure about the spelling, but his name was Kim Yong Kuk. He was a small man, probably in his mid thirties. He was very bright, busy and active, and very comfortable to work with. I really enjoyed talking to him about so many things. I was obviously sufficiently impressed with him to mention him in a letter home:

> The Korean contractor is a little guy that used to work for the Japanese army. He went to college in Japan and can read & write English pretty well. I get a big kick out of talking to him about politics as

he is slightly pro-Japanese. He doesn't come right
out and say so but I can tell from the way he talks.

I really enjoyed talking to Kim Yong Kuk about so many
things. I had often wondered why GI's called the Koreans
"Gooks." The term seemed quite derogatory, but I had a
good enough relationship with Kim to ask him about it.
He told me that the GI's should not be blamed for using
the word. He explained that the Korean word for Chinese
was "Chung-gook" and the word for Americans was "Me-
gook." When the GI's arrived in Korea, the Koreans pointed
to them an called, "Me-gook, Me-gook." The GI's thought
they were telling them that they, the Koreans, were to be
called gooks. I have no idea if Kim's explanation was correct, but it seemed reasonable.

On September 29 and 30 all construction work came to a
virtual halt because the Koreans did not come to work. I
was told that these were the days that the Koreans celebrated Christmas. I never learned how it was celebrated
or if it was a Christmas comparable to the Christmas celebrated in other parts of the Christian world. Judging from
the time of year, it was more likely a harvest festival than a
religious holiday.

The Korean Christmas holiday reminded me that Koreans
workers were also absent from camp shortly after I arrived
in late January. As I mentioned in one of my first letters
home from the Wire Platoon, Koreans celebrated the New
Year on January 20, a day on which all Koreans become
one year older. The New Year holiday called for a whole
week of celebration.

Of all of my contacts with Korean people, one remains very clear in my mind even to this day. It happened on July 20, 1947, on my second one-day pass to Kunsan. At the time it seemed almost like a dream. I wrote home about the experience in the limited language of an unworldly youth:

> I went to Kunsan today with Jones, so for a change I have a little to write about.
>
> We left here about 10 AM on a GI bus (believe it or not). Arrived at Kunsan docks about $^{1}/_{2}$ hour later and started walking toward the main street. The town stunk more than usual due to the hot weather.
>
> We stopped in a tearoom which is not off limits and is located a few blocks from the main street. It was a small, very clean place with a low doorway (5 $^{1}/_{2}$ or 6 ft). Trees and shrubs were growing in pots around the room. The place looked almost Stateside. We had a cup of coffee in there. From there we went up to the main street where Jones got a haircut.
>
> After the haircut we walked over to the KCC building - GI's live there - and ate noon chow. I know the mess sergeant there, so we had no trouble getting fed.
>
> About 1 PM, it started raining and we happened to be walking toward a place where we could get a ride back to camp so we got soaked. It's funny the way this weather is. I was soaked from the rain, yet I was sweating.

Anyway, we spotted a big rich-looking house on a hill so we decided to pay the owners a visit and get out of the rain for a while. Walked up to the house and an old guy invited us in. Jones gave him a cigarette and immediately he was an old friend. The man motioned to us to take off our shoes; we did. Then he showed us around the house.

The floors were paved with straw woven together like a mattress - very soft.

The main room of the place had a shrine in it. There was a gold colored 'Budda' [sic] on a sort of altar. From the ceiling was hanging a gold-colored chandelier about 4 ft in diameter with a lot of fancy metal gadgets hanging on it. There were about 6 places where incense was burning. The place really had an oriental atmosphere.

We bowed and said good-bye to the Korean and walked out to where we left our shoes, put them on, bowed again and left. The bowing is a custom here and as the man treated us very nice we decided to be polite to him.

I have often regretted that I was too young and too restricted in my movements to be able to learn more about the Korean people, their lives, and their culture. However, even while I was there, I often thought of the immense, but wasted, opportunity we had to help the Korean people in their period of great need for food, clothing, housing, and good government.

In 1947, the United States was without question the most successful democracy in modern history. We had played a major role in winning World War II, and were in the process of occupying and guiding the establishment of new governments in countries such as West Germany, Italy, Japan, and South Korea. Even though democratic governments were set up in these countries, none mirrored the strong and successful system of the United States.

It is possible that England and France, because of their roles in the war in Europe, insisted upon parliamentary-type governments in both Italy and West Germany. However, in the case of Japan and South Korea, America was the major occupying power. Why was the American system not used as a model? I often thought, as I looked at Korea from my position as a foot soldier, that the best gift that we could have ever given to the South Korean people was our Constitution and Bill of Rights.

CHAPTER SIXTEEN

WAITING FOR ORDERS

My work routine continued to be essentially the same until the day I left Camp Hillenmeyer. The only change that occurred was that my letters home spoke less of my daily activities and more of my return trip.

In the last month or two, I thought a great deal about going home. By Christmas I was expecting orders for the trip home at any moment. However, I had started writing about my return as early as July and, by August, I was making plans for the trip home:

> Don't send me any of the pictures I took over here. I'll wait 'til I get home. I'm a 'short timer' now. The most I can have is 5 months. The latest I can leave here is the middle of January.

> I don't think I'll be home for Xmas, but I may. A lot of things can happen in 5 months.

From that time on, one letter expressed the belief that I would be home by Christmas and the next that I would not:

> I guess it's O.K. to send me a Christmas package as I don't expect to leave here until Jan 15th. Also don't hold up Christmas for me because I might not get home until March.

By November 20 I had something definite to report:

> The roster with my name and 800 other names was submitted to the 1st Repple Depot today. I am about 400th on the list. The next roster I'm on will be the one that reassigns me to the Zone of Interior (home).

> I don't think I'll make the Dec 11th ship. I'll probably get the Republic on the 30th of Dec or one along there, as there is a ship leaving about every other day from Jan 1 to Jan 15. Anyway, there is no use worrying about it. The orders will come in due time — for sure after Xmas. I figure on spending a white Xmas here in the Land of Rice and Honey Carts.

In late November we heard some disconcerting news from friends at the Replacement Depot at Yongdungp'o, the staging facility through which all enlisted army personnel entering and leaving South Korea had to pass. I relayed the information to my parents:

> Yongdungp'o is something that everybody dreads around here. That place is really a hole. We heard

from some of the guys that were here and are on their way home. They left here at 4:30 AM. At noon they arrived in Iri — 21 miles away from here. 36 hours after that they reached Yongdungp'o, which is about 150 miles from Iri. Pretty good trains they have around here.

It's way overcrowded up there, the chow is very scarce and there are no stoves. One guy that used to sleep in the hut here had to sleep outside while he was up there. It's a good thing we'll only have to stay there 2 or 3 days. I'll have to take more than a candy bar with me to keep from getting hungry.

Because of the news of conditions in Yongdungp'o, I started preparing for my trip home in early December,

You asked me if I was going to carry a big duffel bag back with me. Yes, but it won't be very full. I'm going to turn everything in I won't need right here. There is no use dragging all the worn out stuff I have back to the States.

Anyway we have to leave most everything here so the replacements that never arrive will have something to wear when they get here.

I'm starting to stock up on candy bars and cookies from the PX. I know that when I hit the Reppel Depot it will be so crowded that we'll be lucky if we get any chow at all. Most of all don't worry as I can take care of myself.

On December 24, I made note of the cold weather and gave a list of ships that, hopefully, included the one that would bring me home:

> You say the weather at home is cold. You should see it here. Everything is frozen. We even have frost on the toilet seats.

> I don't think I will sail on the Republic. Right now I don't know exactly what's going on. All I can do is wait. Here's a list of ships leaving in the near future:

> Republic - Jan 2
> Frederick Funston - Jan 5
> General Brewster - Jan 6
> Hope - Jan 15
> General Greely - Jan 22
> General Aultman - Jan 24
> Comfort - Jan 24
> General Hodges - Jan 26
> General Haan - Feb 10
> General Blatchford - Feb 24

> Your guess is as good as mine.

In early January, I was still awaiting orders:

> Here it is Jan 7 and I'm still here, and the way things look now I don't expect to leave for another month or more. I think we are going to stay here until the last minute.

No use writing to me because it will be at least 30 days before your letter can get here. The mail system is in terrible shape. No mail has come thru for a week. The Korean trains are getting worse all the time. It takes 3 or 4 days to get to Seoul (150 mi) now.

Ten days later, on January 17, disaster struck Camp Hillenmeyer:

I wasn't going to write anymore until my orders came down, but we had a little excitement the other nite so I thought I'd tell you about it.

Our new hospital burned to the ground Saturday nite about midnite. The hospital was just finished and was in use only about a month.

Here's what happened. Everybody in the hut came in drunk except Mills and I. We finally got in bed about 11 PM after much commotion.

I was just getting to sleep when one of the guys heard a bell ringing. He looked out the window and noticed the fire as the hospital is just across the road. I was still awake so I got up and we woke up most of the guys. Some of them were passed out.

I got dressed in a big hurry and ran over. I got there about the same time the [Camp Hillenmeyer's] fire truck did. The place was all in flames and the 7 or 8 patients were out so we didn't try to go in.

The guy that sleeps on one side of me was about 20 sheets in the wind and still had his clothes on when he found out about the fire. He ran right over and inside the place and almost got overcome by smoke. Mills and I carried him back to the hut as he kept staggering toward the fire.

Just as we got him to the hut, Capt. Lutz (Post Engineer) came in all excited looking for bulldozer drivers. There weren't any around so Mills and I grabbed the closest jeep and went after Case. He sleeps in the warehouse near the double hangar and is the heavy equipment foreman. We came storming in and found him sober and still up. He thought we came down to wake him up and tip his bed over. He wouldn't believe us so we dragged him outside and showed him the blaze.

The word spread that bulldozer operators were needed so by the time we got to where they were parked, 20 or 30 drunks were milling around claiming they were cat operators. It was really funny.

I wanted to see the fire so I went back. There are no fire hydrants in camp so the fire truck had to haul all the water used on the fire.

The bulldozer is what really stopped the fire. The corridor it crashed thru was already in flames. The dozer was driven by Louie Downs of Fresno Calif.

Meanwhile the GI fire truck from Kunsan was on its way. It made it out here in 15 minutes which is

a record. It usually takes 40 minutes without loaf-
ing. The reason for the speed was that the driver
was so drunk he could hardly walk. When it got
here the pump on it was frozen so the truck was of
no use.

After the fire I worked in the drafting office. We had the
job of drawing maps of the hospital for the reports and in-
vestigations of the fire. The burned out area consisted of a
large ward, the operating room, orderly room, dispensary,
dental clinic, and the x-ray laboratory (where we developed our photographs).

A few ward buildings in the western area of the hospital
compound were saved by the bulldozer breaking through
the corridor that separated them from the burning buildings in the eastern area.

There was no effort to rebuild the hospital during the balance of the time I was at Camp Hillenmeyer. In fact, a decision of which we were totally unaware had apparently
already been made to close the camp and turn it over to
Korean Constabulary forces (the South Korean Army).

On February 3rd I was still awaiting orders and observing
all of the activity in camp:

So far my orders have not come down so I'm still
here until further notice; altho I expect to leave any
week now. The suspense is killing me.

The number of men around here is getting pretty
small. The whole 2nd Bn has only about 200 men

in it. F & G Companies are being replaced with Korean Constabulary.

About 400 Korean soldiers are going to move into F & G Co's Thursday. They are going to pull guard and other duties that will make it easier on the GI's.

The camp is finally going to close up and the 63rd deactivated. In spite of everything there aren't enough men to hold the camp so the 1st & 20th Inf. and the 18-monthers will go home.

P.E. is building boxes like mad as everything has to be crated and shipped out. The place is supposed to be vacant by the end of March.

P.E. is in a big confusion. Koreans are running around all over the place. They are learning to drive trucks and cats so they can take our places. We have a Korean draftsman now. That's why we aren't doing anything. He's doing all the work.

By this time, my family was beginning to wonder if something was terribly wrong. All of the friends who had enlisted with me, Bill, George, Parker, and Bob, had returned home by Christmas. They had been discharged several months before the end of their enlistment periods.

All I could tell my folks, in response to their letters asking why I had not yet been discharged, was that my friends had been stationed in Japan, and that men who went to Korea were treated differently than those who went to Japan.

Even today, history books add only that the army had been dismantled too rapidly after World War II, so that by 1948 manpower shortages were severe, particularly in Korea. The Korean situation was exacerbated by the fact that Congress considered the occupation of Korea a waste of money. Thus, the army was forced to delay, for as long as possible, the departure of those troops that were already Korea. As a result, no one in Korea was discharged before the end of his enlistment period.

On February 8th I sent home the very welcome news:

> I'm coming home!!! It's hard to believe but it's true. We're supposed to be at Yongdungp'o Tues the 10th of Feb. We won't make it in time because the orders came too late. We will probably leave here Tuesday.

> The first I heard of it was last nite when Mette walked in and told me that he saw my orders at the message center. You know Mette I think. I met him the first day I came in the army; he got sworn in with me. He works on the Kunsan switchboard so he gets all the inside dope. Actually the orders didn't come down until noon today.

> By the way, Mette is on the same orders. He's been with me all the way thru the army so far. We got the official poop today when a guy from personnel told us.

> There are four of us going from this hut. J.D. Pauley, Winton, Carroll, and I. The only thing is they leave

the day after me. I hope they get the same ship.
The guys are really happy. I didn't think four guys
could make such a commotion.

That was my last letter from Camp Hillenmeyer.

CHAPTER SEVENTEEN

GOING HOME

We left Camp Hillenmeyer by truck on the morning of February 11, 1948, to go to the train station in Iri, about 25 miles to the east of Kunsan via a dirt road. There were about six on the truck.

The train we were to take to Yongdungp'o was one that made the trip daily between Pusan and Seoul, making numerous stops along the way. The train had one troop car between the locomotive and the civilian passenger cars which, as usual, were full. The troop car was uncrowded and fairly comfortable even though it was already occupied by 10-15 enlisted men that had boarded the train sometime earlier, before it arrived at Iri.

As evening approached and it started to get dark, we began to wonder how we would know when we arrived at Yongdungp'o. We could not read the station signs. Eventually a Korean conductor came into our car and said, "GI's off here." When the train stopped, we got off the train into a snowstorm. There was about a foot of snow on the ground.

It was pitch dark. There did not seem to be a station there or even a town nearby, but there was a small shack about six feet square that was lit inside by a single electric bulb. We began to wonder if the conductor knew what he was doing when he put us off the train.

After shivering a while, we walked over to the small shack and rattled the window. The station agent opened the window and we asked, "Yongdungp'o?" to which he replied, "OK, OK." So again we waited in the snow.

After a while it occurred to us that perhaps we had not made ourselves understood, so we rattled the window again. When the agent opened his window this time, the small crowd of soldiers made clear with gestures and shouts that he, the agent, would very soon be physically attacked if he did not call somebody. Because the agent apparently spoke no English, all he could say was, "OK, OK, OK," and then we saw him pick up his telephone and speak to someone in the Korean language.

Finally after about an hour we heard a distant roar of engines that could only come from army trucks. The trucks eventually arrived. They were six-by-sixes without the usual canvas covers. The ride to the First Replacement Depot, located near Yongdungp'o, took about 20 minutes.

I do not recall seeing anything of interest along the way. All I remember is that it was a miserably cold and windy ride in the back of that truck. The trucks dropped us off in an empty field covered with hard-packed snow. We received no instructions other than to wait there. We were joined later by more GI's that came from somewhere we did not know. Sometime after midnight, a sergeant came to greet us with the news that the depot was totally full and that we would have to sleep in the customs shakedown building.

The shakedown building was a wooden structure on a wooden platform with wooden walls about four feet high. From there to the roof the walls were open screening. We had lots of fresh air that night. It was so cold I could not sleep, even though I kept on all the clothes I wore on the trip, including my necktie.

The day before leaving Camp Hillenmeyer, we had turned in all our warm outer clothing, parkas and snowpacks (cold weather boots), and were issued standard wool overcoats. For the trip to Yongdungp'o I wore long johns, a standard olive drab wool uniform, leather combat boots, and the wool overcoat.

My last letter as an enlisted man was sent from Yongdungp'o on Friday, February 13, 1948:

Arrived at Yongdungp'o Wednesday nite about 11:30 PM. They packed us up in trucks and took us to the Repl. Depot. The place was overcrowded, so about 35 of us had to sleep in the building where the customs shakedown is given. It was the coldest night I've ever spent in Korea, We slept on canvas cots with only 2 GI wool blankets. It got so cold about 4 AM that a couple of us got up and stayed in the guard house until morning.

We got processed starting at 8 AM. First we got a customs shakedown, which was a laugh. We took everything out of our bags, put it in a big pile, the inspector walks by, and we pack again.

We exchanged our occupation currency today for real U.S. money. Does it look good.

The reason we went to the guard house that first cold and sleepless night was because we asked ourselves where we might find a warm place to wait for processing. The logical answer was the guard house.

It was the wrong answer — the guard house was stone cold. It was in a large room at one end of an old Japanese barracks, with a stove, but no fire, and double deck steel bunks with springs, but no mattresses or blankets. I wondered to myself what ever happened to the roomful of mattresses we found the last time I was here.

There were a couple of off-duty guards standing around the stone-cold stove talking and one hardy soul sound asleep on metal springs with no blankets at all. We asked the guards if the sleeping fellow was drunk. They replied that he was not, but rather he was just a person who could sleep anywhere. It struck me that here was a perfect example of the great variability among members of the human race.

The First Replacement Depot at Yongdungp'o seemed little changed from when I passed through it more than a year earlier. It was a bleak, cold place in winter, in a snow-covered valley surrounded by fairly steep snow-covered hills. The trees and shrubs were devoid of leaves, and the structures, almost all Japanese military barracks, were low and unpainted and had a dark gray look. There was absolutely no color. Every vista was like a scene painted in shades of gray, with occasional splashes of black, on a white background. To me it looked cold and dismal, not a place that one would find inviting.

After that first cold night we were transferred to a low, windowless building for the balance of our short stay at Yongdungp'o. It was warm and comfortable and I slept well there, except for the twenty-four hours of fire guard duty assigned to me by the bulletin board.

The fire guard job in this instance was to attend a wood-fired stove in a building under construction. The concrete floor in the building was freshly poured and, in order prevent the concrete from being damaged by freezing while it was hardening, a fire was kept going in the building around the clock. I was on duty three hours and off duty six hours for a period of 24 hours.

While returning to my barracks early on a dark, cold morning after my last three-hour stint, I inadvertently stepped into a ditch of ice cold water up to my waist. It was one of the many drainage ditches in the camp. The water was covered by a thin layer of ice on top of which was a foot or more of fresh snow. The snow hid the nature of the ground underneath and, as usual, nobody bothered to tell the new-comers about such pitfalls. I slogged back to the barracks, hung my clothes up to dry, and climbed into bed.

Despite the same outward bleak appearance, the Replace-ment Depot had actually changed quite a bit in the months since I had been there. There were more western-style buildings that had been erected by the U.S. Army, includ-ing new wooden barracks buildings and a large, low build-ing used as a mess hall. However, one thing that had not changed was the soft, sticky earth that covered the roads and walkways. I commented in my last letter home:

> This camp is really a mud hole in the afternoon when the sun thaws out the ice. My shoes were really polished when I got here but you ought to see them now.

I cannot remember much about other events of my very short stay at Yongdungp'o, except for some sort of mini-mal processing and the usual short-arm inspection.

Two days after my arrival at Yongdungp'o my name ap-peared on the roster of men scheduled to leave for Inch'on and the U.S. Army Transport General Haan on Saturday, February 14.

The good news was included in my last letter home:

> We are sailing on the General Haan Saturday, the 14th, if things go as they are. I don't know where it's going or when it hits the States. There are a lot of guys here I came overseas with. It sure is good

to see them again. I hope they will be on the same
ship as I am.

We left for Inch'on by truck, then were transferred to a train.
When all were gathered on the dock at Inch'on harbor waiting to board the General Haan, we numbered about 1300.
We were put into some sort of formation and marked with
big chalk letters and numbers on our backpacks. We were
cautioned not to mill around, but to keep our places so we
would not mix up our numbers. Dutifully, we walked in
proper order, trying to abide by the rules, and boarded a
waiting LST.

LST stands for Landing Ship Tank, many of which were
built for the seaborne invasions of World War II. An LST is
a big ship, 200-300 feet long and about 50 feet wide, with a
large superstructure at the rear. It has an open main deck
about 30 feet above the waterline, with an internal ramp
leading from the main deck to the lower deck.

The lower deck looks like a large, long garage. It has clam-
shell doors that form the prow of the ship when closed.
Behind these doors is an inner door, hinged at the bottom,
that can be let down to form a ramp for unloading mobile
equipment on an invasion beach. LSTs are capable of traveling on the open ocean, but also can run in shallow water
and up on a beach.

The LST we boarded easily accommodated all 1300 of us,
with about half the group, including me, on the open main
deck and the other half in the lower deck. It took us to the
General Haan, which was at anchor about 20 miles away
in the outer harbor. The day was gray, cold, and overcast,

just like the one that greeted us on arrival a little more than a year before.

I stayed on the top deck of the LST, along with 500-600 others, peering out through the overcast. As the LST was moving out into the outer harbor, we noticed a Korean junk (a Chinese-style wooden sailing ship) moving toward us. We watched in disbelief as the junk stayed its course. It eventually side-swiped us, and its sails and ropes became entangled with the railing and lower rigging of the LST. We stopped. The two vessels were stuck fast together.

Some of the GI's on deck became upset by the possibility that this delay might somehow interfere with the long-awaited trip home. Almost instantly, without waiting for the LST's crew to attend to the problem, a dozen or so GI's on the top deck attacked the junk's ropes and sails with pocket knives, cutting them and freeing the LST. The ships parted and we moved on, leaving a disabled junk drifting in our wake.

Finally the General Haan came into view. Our LST pulled up alongside and a Jacob's ladder was lowered in the midst of us. We stood obediently in the proper order, waiting for our sergeant to give the order to board. The silence was broken by a loudspeaker on the General Haan shouting, "OK everyone get aboard." A moment of puzzlement followed and then a mild panic broke out. We all rushed helter-skelter for the ladder.

For some unknown and irrational reason we had been suddenly possessed with the fear of being left behind. There went our orderly formation — our chalk marks were all mixed together. But no one seemed to care. Once aboard, we followed directions from the crew of the General Haan. The weather was cold and overcast with a brisk north wind that chilled us to the bone.

As I stood on the deck of the troop ship looking back at the gray skies and colorless Inch'on skyline, many thoughts went through my mind. I could not believe that this day had finally arrived and that I was on my way home, back to California. During the entire time in Korea, many of my friends and I were haunted by the fear that we would never leave Korea alive. My tremendous relief at having escaped with my life provoked an emotion that faded with the passage of time, but which I still remember with remarkable clarity: "One thing for sure, I never want to set foot in this God-forsaken place ever again."

Below deck, the layout of the General Haan was somewhat similar to that of Eufaula Victory, except that the compartments in the General Haan were smaller and there were many more passageways. The Eufaula Victory was built as a cargo ship and converted to a troop transport by filling its huge, undivided cargo holds with floor to ceiling tiers of bunks.

The General Haan, on the other hand, was originally designed and built as a troop ship. Its troop carrying capacity was about the same as that of the Eufaula Victory, but it was more compact. The General Haan was no faster, seemed more crowded, and was less comfortable than that old converted cargo freighter, the Eufaula Victory.

Above deck, the ships were very different. The General Haan had a massive superstructure with an open deck about ten feet wide skirting the perimeter of the ship. There were no wide hatch covers or wide expanse of deck to lay one's self down on and gaze up at the sky, as there were on the Eufaula Victory. There was no comfortable place on the General Haan to see the sights.

It was also not easy to get from one side of the ship to the other. To do so, one had to walk all the way around the front or back of the ship, or go below and through compartments and passageways to come up on the other side. As a result, I spent very little time on deck on the trip home.

There was not much seasickness on the way home. The ocean was calm for most of the trip, and we met with no huge ground swells like those so common in the waters outside of San Francisco Bay. Some of us felt a little queasy at times, but there was nothing we could not handle.

Our first stop was Naha, Okinawa. Here was one of the few times I went on deck. The scene was very much like that at Agaña, Guam. There was a lot of debris and evidence of damage all around. Also like Guam, we were given no information about why we had stopped and were not allowed off the ship. We assumed our stop at Naha was to pick up fuel and supplies and perhaps a few civilians.

After leaving Naha, we sailed around the southern tip of the island to Buckner Bay to pick up a contingent of about 300 Marines. The bay was named in honor of General Simon Bolivar Buckner, who was Commander of the Tenth Army that invaded Okinawa on April 1, 1945. General

Buckner was killed on June 18, 1945, while overseeing final mop-up operations against the Japanese who had been
pushed into the southernmost area of the Island.

Buckner Bay held quite a sight. There was a causeway several hundred or more feet long, that lead out to the wharves.
This causeway had been built on a foundation of trucks,
jeeps, tanks, and every other kind of military equipment.
The top of the causeway was covered with several feet of
packed dirt to form a roadway, but the sides exposed the
nature of the foundation. It had obviously been hastily built
under combat conditions to improve the ability to supply
troops fighting the fierce battles that took place at the southern tip of Okinawa. The causeway was an impressive and
almost unbelievable picture.

The marines who came aboard at Buchner Bay were quartered apart from the rest of us. I would have liked to talk
with them, but was not able to. We never saw them except
when they were standing guard. They guarded everything
aboard ship, the brig, entrances to various doors, and other
places around the ship that did not appear to need guarding. It seemed to me that it was a make-work program for
the marines, just to keep them busy. They were to be admired, though. They all looked very professional — neat
and clean and polished. They did not talk to or fraternize
with the army personnel aboard.

For us, there was no organization aboard ship. We all wandered around, filling our time as best we could. I sensed
that the coming weeks of trip would seem very long. There
was no point to writing letters now because I would be
home before the letters arrived. And there was a limit to

reading and talking. Thus, after a few days at sea, I went to the troop office to volunteer for some job, preferably in or near the mess — other than KP. I explained that I had worked in a butcher shop after school and had learned how to cut meat. I was told to come back the next day.

The next day I was assigned to the meat department storeroom located in the center of the ship, four levels below the main deck. I carried boxes of meat out of the refrigerator to be delivered to the cooks. In addition to meat, I got other staples out of the storeroom for transfer to the kitchen: cheese, eggs, apples, oranges, and so forth. My job also included emptying garbage cans. I never had to cut meat, but that did not bother me — I had a lot to eat.

I worked only four hours a day. In addition to a short work day, the job brought me more benefits than I had anticipated. I not only had a job to occupy some time but I was also off the KP list. I could have my fill of apples and oranges and, best of all, I could go to the front of the chow line at every meal.

The chow lines on the General Haan were notorious for their length. Those at the end of a line had to wait literally hours for their meals. My white mess jacket was my ticket to a place in the front of the line. Toward the end of the trip there seemed to be less work for me to do, but my privileges remained.

We came under the Golden Gate Bridge and into San Francisco Bay on an overcast day. Everyone went on deck to watch our approach to the dock at Fort Mason, which is located in San Francisco near the Golden Gate Bridge. The ship actually listed to one side because of the weight of all the soldiers who had crowded to the side of the ship facing toward land. When the ship docked, we were sent below to pick up our belongings. Then we waited our turn to leave the ship and plant our feet on home soil.

Civilians, officers, and dependents left the ship first. When and where the marines debarked we did not know. They were nowhere to be seen when our turn to leave came. After we went down the gangplank, we walked along the dock to a waiting ferryboat that would take us to Camp Stoneman. It was the same former Key System ferry boat, the Yerba Buena, that had carried us from Camp Stoneman to the Oakland Army Base more than a year earlier.

Camp Stoneman had also changed while I was in Korea. It had been constructed as a port of embarkation during World War II. When I returned, it was serving as a separation center where troops from overseas were being processed and discharged, and it would soon be closed.

Our arrival at Camp Stoneman was uneventful. We were taken to a group of empty, two-story wooden barracks buildings and, as before, told to watch the bulletin board. Not much happened. We were assigned to KP several times, but otherwise there was no movement. We arrived during the first week of March, but then had to wait for two weeks before our separation process began.

As the time passed, I became increasingly concerned because my enlistment ended on March 23, 1948 and I was anxious to return home to register for the spring semester at Santa Rosa Junior College. The semester had begun on

March 1, and every day that I wasted at Camp Stoneman meant that I might get home too late to be admitted to the spring semester.

Finally, on March 22, the processing for our separation began. We moved in a long line through various stations. At one of these stops, uniforms and shoes in acceptable condition were issued to those who needed them for the trip home. At other stops, our records were checked and our identities verified. The last stop was at a window where we were presented with any pay owed us plus sufficient money to pay for one-way travel home.

At this point it was late in the afternoon of March 23. According to my calculations, the Army had kept me three hours past the end of my enlistment. I was supposed to be a free man, but I was still in an army facility. I received my final pay and was told by the paymaster I was all finished and could go home. He pointed to a door that said EXIT.

When I reached the door, a burly sergeant was blocking it. I said, "Excuse me, I'm discharged." He pointed to another door with a sign that said ARMY RESERVES. He told me I could not go out through his door but would have to go through the army reserve door.

I do not recall his exact words because, by this time, I was very angry and upset. Regardless of what words he used, they told me, in effect, that I would have to sign up for the reserves in order to leave the facility. Others behind me in line simply followed the sergeant's orders.

I felt intimidated by this sergeant, because all of my experience in the army told me that one did not disobey any superior, yet to sign up for the reserves was more than I could bring myself to do at that point in my life.

I went over to a nearby bench to sit down and review my situation. The army had not reasonably fed, clothed, or trained me. I had a persistent, uncomfortable skin disease and I had nearly lost all my teeth due to malnutrition. I decided that I would risk court martial, a jail term, or whatever punishment the army would impose, rather than commit myself to service in the army reserves. With that I got up and went back to the exit door.

I went up to the sergeant and told him that there was no law that required me to sign up for the reserves. He mumbled something while continuing to direct others to the army reserve door. A short while later, he moved slightly away from the exit and I slipped past him out into the fresh air. I was very relieved and pleased to be free and on my way home.

It should be mentioned here that my repugnance for reserve status was not a lasting one. Many years later, upon receiving a Masters of Public Health degree from the University of California, Berkeley, I became a reserve officer in the U.S. Public Health Service Commissioned Corps.

After escaping from the clutches of the sergeant at Camp Stoneman, I boarded a Greyhound bus bound for Santa Rosa. I remember getting off the bus, taking a taxi for the few miles to our house, walking up the steps of the side porch, opening the door, and calling out, "I'm home." I recall nothing about my reception, other than my mother, father, and brother were there to greet me.

Many years later, my brother told me that on my return, my father's behavior toward me was totally changed; he appeared to regard me as another adult in the home and no longer one of the children. My brother also told me that, on the other hand, my mother was filled with child-like joy at my return. Her boy was home. I was the same Fritz — the name she called me throughout her life — that had left the home a year and a half before. Now she could relax and not worry about me anymore.

This ends the personal account of my life as a soldier in the Army of Occupation in South Korea during 1947 and early 1948.

CHAPTER EIGHTEEN

LOOKING BACK

The year 1948 found me entering a new and happier phase of life. I left the army and returned to school. At the same time, the turmoil in South Korea continued and her fortunes worsened. United States occupation forces, with the exception of about 600 military advisors, were withdrawn. Shortly thereafter, the country became a battleground. What follows here are two stories, both briefly told: The first is mine, and the second is that of Korea.

Upon arriving home, I found that the spring semester at our local junior college was already four weeks old. I was depressed by the thought that I would have to wait until the fall semester started before I could return to school. But that was army thinking. I had forgotten what an informal, friendly place Northern California was in 1948. The registrar at Santa Rosa Junior College, Ms. Hallberg, was most helpful to me. She suggested that I register late and work with my instructors to make up the four weeks of school that I had missed.

My friends, Bill Brandt, George Doka, and Parker Hall, were also of great help. They had been discharged several months earlier and, thus, were able to start the semester on time. They were concerned about my late arrival, so they saved their class notes and completed homework assignments to help me in making up for lost time.

By February 1949, I had completed my second of two years at the Junior College and was admitted to the School of Chemical Engineering at Stanford University. Parker, Bill, and George also transferred to major universities. Parker and Bill were admitted to Stanford in the Schools of Civil Engineering and Mechanical Engineering, respectively, and George went to the Civil Engineering School at the University of Oregon. Bob Larsen did not to go on to a four-year college after graduation from Santa Rosa Junior College, but instead decided to return to the family farm.

The GI Bill made a major difference in our lives. Without it, we probably would not have been able to obtain college educations. None of us had parents who could afford to pay the costs of attending an out-of-town university. The benefits that I had earned from the GI Bill were adequate to pay tuition, books, and room and board for a period of 30 months at Stanford. This was sufficient time for me to earn a Bachelor of Science Degree in Chemical Engineering.

I worked summers to earn additional spending money. My summer work was a continuation of what I did in Korea. Skilled land surveying crew members were always in demand, so I always had a summer job waiting at home in the Santa Rosa area of California.

In retrospect, the GI Bill turned out to be of tremendous value, not only to its recipients but also to the United States in general. Many people who never could have afforded a four-year college education were able to earn degrees of their choices.

The skeptics who said that the GI Bill would flood the country with over-educated people and that there would be too many doctors, lawyers, teachers, and engineers were wrong. The GI Bill came at the right time to provide the nation with the skilled people necessary to win the cold war and to lead and take advantage of the major advances in technology that occurred in the second half of the 20th century.

Perhaps more important to me personally, the GI Bill changed American attitudes about who should go to college. Before World War II, the formal education of the average young person ended with graduation from high school. College student populations around the nation were relatively small. The huge increase in number of college students caused by the GI Bill did not shrink to the levels of former days after the program ended. Instead, college populations remained at the higher levels and then increased after the war veterans graduated.

The GI Bill demonstrated that higher education was not an unattainable goal reserved for an elite few who aspired to be physicians or professors. The lessons of the GI Bill were that everybody who had the will to learn could succeed in college and that higher education was an important way of making one's future more interesting and more secure.

After being home only a short time, it became obvious to me that my time in the army had actually been a positive experience, despite the misery I suffered at the time. I realized how fortunate I was to have been born in the United States. I felt school was a privilege and worked harder. I had more concern for other people. The behavior of some people in authority had taught me the foolishness of feelings of self-importance. I revered my freedom as an American citizen because, as a soldier, I had learned what it was like to have no rights and no freedom. And, the GI Bill was making it possible for me to earn a college degree.

The chemical engineering program at Stanford was extremely difficult. It covered a wide range of demanding subjects from chemistry and engineering to the German language. I had almost no time to do anything except study. But this was also a good time in my life. I enjoyed chemical engineering. I enjoyed learning about boilers, furnaces, fluid flow, electrical machinery, and designing chemical plants and oil refineries.

I lived in Stanford Village, a huge living complex, along with about 1000 other veterans. Stanford Village had formerly housed the Dibble General Hospital, a U.S. Army Hospital that had been declared surplus at the end of World War II. It was located in the City of Menlo Park, about four miles from the Stanford campus.

Stanford was a friendly place with nice people, both students and faculty. An example of the friendliness of the time was a ride-sharing program between the campus and off-campus living units. Students without automobiles never needed to walk or take buses to and from school.

They were always picked up by students who owned cars. Those with cars stopped at the entrance to Stanford Village to take students without cars to campus. They also stopped at a pickup station on campus to give them a lift home.

While I was still at Stanford, in 1950, the Korean War began. My very good friend, Bill, was recalled into the army and had to leave school. During our time in the service, Bill had been stationed in Japan where conditions were such that he felt good enough about the army to sign up for the Army Reserves. Shortly after his recall, Bill was sent to Korea. He then spent a year or more in the front lines. Fortunately, he was not injured. He came back to Stanford and graduated several years later than he had originally planned.

After Bill's experience, I often thought about the laws of chance and how they affect one's life. The roll of the dice that sent me to the misery of Korea sent Bill to a decent army unit in Japan. Those chance occurrences resulted in personal decisions about the military that had profound effects on our later lives.

After graduating, I worked as a process engineer for a half dozen years at a major oil company. I enjoyed the work, which included redesigning and operating petroleum refining plants. Like other fields of engineering, chemical engineers build things and have the pleasure of seeing their work take shape in concrete and steel in the form of towers, furnaces, pipes, pumps, and tanks. Probably what is less known to the general public is that a more important pleasure to chemical engineers is to see their new plants start up and reliably produce quality products at low cost.

After leaving the oil refinery, I decided to apply my chemical engineering education to the profession of industrial hygiene, which is the control of chemicals and other factors in the work environment that may cause illness among workers. In short, the major activity of the industrial hygiene profession is the prevention of diseases of occupations by means of engineering control of the work environment. I eventually went back to school, this time to the University of California, Berkeley, and earned Master of Public Health and Ph.D. degrees in industrial hygiene. I enjoyed this profession until my retirement.

Korea, when I departed in 1948, was a little more than two years away from a major war. Had I not enlisted in the army when I did and served my time in the military, I would certainly have been drafted and perhaps would not have survived the Korean War, a war that killed 33,629 American military personnel and wounded another 103,284. Listed as missing or captured were another 5,178 Americans. In addition, the Korean War destroyed many more United Nations soldiers, Korean soldiers and civilians, and caused enemy casualties exceeding 1.5 million.

Had it not been for the Korean War, I probably would not have thought seriously again about the army and my experiences in South Korea. But, the narrow margin by which I missed the Korean War made me think again about the soldiers who were killed or injured in that suffering land and wonder why such sacrifice occurred.

In 1948, prior to the start of the war, the American forces in South Korea were the last outpost of the free world on the

Asian mainland. North of the 38th parallel on the Korean Peninsula was the Peoples Republic of Korea. Touching the northern border of this small, but militant, Communist country were the borders of the Peoples Republic of China (Communist China) and the Soviet Union. If lost to the Communists, South Korea would serve as an ideal jumping off point for the invasion of Japan.

It is obvious the United States, at some point, recognized the strategic importance of South Korea because the United States immediately came to South Korea's defense when the Korean war started. This immediate move to defend South Korea raises some interesting questions about American policies.

Why did the United States fail to recognize the strategic importance of South Korea earlier and improve both the image and the strength of American occupation forces in South Korea? Why were the occupation forces so badly managed? Why did food, clothing, and armaments fail to reach the occupation forces? What was the objective of the United States Army in occupying South Korea? Why did the United States remove the last of its occupation forces in 1949, only a year before the Korean War started?

Retirement has given me time to reflect on these questions and my experiences in that unfortunate country. It also gave me time to read more extensively about Korea and the aftermath of World War II. A list of books I found very useful in my quest for understanding, some of which are referred to in this and preceding chapters, is included in Appendix B. I recommend this list to anyone interested in learning more about the history of the period and the political situation affecting South Korea at that time

The major players in the Asian theater in 1948 were the United States, the Soviet Union, and China. The Soviet Union and the United States had changed from wartime allies to peacetime enemies. The cold war was starting. President Truman had concluded that the Chinese Nationalist Government of China was a corrupt failure and had no hope of holding mainland China against the Communists.

History supports Truman's conclusion. By 1947, the Communist Chinese were well on their way to driving the Nationalists out of mainland China and forcing them to set up a government on the island of Formosa (Taiwan). For all practical purposes, by the end of 1948, the Communists controlled the Chinese mainland. For an interesting insight into the leadership of the Chinese Nationalist Government, see *The Stilwell Papers* edited by Theodore White.

During the immediate post-World War II period, within the American government, there were strong differences of opinion as to what our foothold in South Korea actually meant. Some felt South Korea should be fortified and defended by American troops because it was the key to protecting Japan against invasion by the Communists. Others felt the American military was too costly and South Korea should be abandoned to save money. Still others felt that South Korea should be held for use in the near future as a staging area for a combined Nationalist Chinese/American war against Communist China. The United States Congress, strongly influenced by the Republican members and the so-called "China Lobby," demanded that we support

was related to an uncertain American foreign policy caused by powerful and rapidly moving world events. President Roosevelt died in April 1945. Vice President Truman, although an extremely able person, inherited a cabinet that was not enamored of him and was generally uncooperative. To make matters worse, with the end of World War II, Congress was demanding an end to the draft and cuts in the budget for the armed forces. The result was that the draft ended and all draftees were released in 1947. As of June 30, 1947, army ground forces had been reduced to a total of 684,000 troops, about 10 divisions, as contrasted with 8 million troops and 89 divisions in 1945 at the end of World War II. In short, the American army was no longer a potent deterrent to any country contemplating war with the United States.

By late 1946, the Soviet Union, our former ally until the end of the war in 1945, had changed into a cold-war enemy. A Soviet blockade of Berlin in 1948 forced the United States into a massive airlift to keep from being driven from the city. And by 1949, as the result of Soviet expansionist policy at that time, the United States was providing military and other aid to Greece, Turkey, Iran, China, Korea, the Philippines, and a number of countries in Latin America.

The pressures generated by all these rapidly moving events led to an official foreign policy that could be interpreted to mean that the United States would not go to war to defend South Korea. In January 1950, about five months before the start of the Korean War, Dean Acheson, Secretary of State, publicly defined the United States defense line in Asia as, "Running south from the Aleutian Islands to Japan, to the Rykukyu Islands, and then to the Philippines." (Matloff, page 544). This statement placed Korea and Taiwan out-side of the defense perimeter of the United States.

According to Acheson, the defense of Korea or Taiwan would require the commitment of the entire world by means of of an affirmative vote in the United Nations be-fore the United States would go to war. The North Kore-ans and the Soviet Union must have interpreted this state-ment as part of a long chain of evidence that the the United States was not particularly concerned about South Korea and, in the event it were invaded, would be unwilling to fight. Contrary to its stated policy, when South Korea was actually invaded, the United States responded quickly and directly using its own troops. It also sought and gained United Nations support.

My own experience, along with the written history of the last fifty years, leads me to believe that the problems that I witnessed in South Korea were early symptoms of a long period of decay in both American foreign policy and Ameri-can military power that lasted into the early 1980's.

The best evidence of this decay can be seen in the origins and the outcomes of the two major American wars that were fought after the end of World War II. The Korean War, which started in 1950, did not end in victory despite claims to the contrary. After prolonged negotiations, it ended in a standoff in which American prisoners were never ad-equately accounted for. Its start was ostensibly a surprise.

Neither the American State Department, intelligence agen-cies, nor the military were prepared for or even alert to the possibility of a full-scale invasion from North Korea. In short, it was another Pearl Harbor, less than ten years after the real Pearl Harbor — a surprise attack that we, as a country, had vowed would never be allowed to be repeated. Bruce Cumings' Volume II of *The Origins of the Korean War* presents an interestingly written, detailed review of the events leading up to the Korean War.

I believe the decay in American foreign policy and military power continued to its climax with the futile pursuit of the Vietnam War and our eventual withdrawal, again without victory, and again without adequate accounting for and return of our prisoners.

War comes to countries that are weak or incompetent, and the losers are the soldiers whose lives are wasted and the citizens whose standard of living is lowered by the economic costs of war. Hopefully the bitter lessons of Korea and Vietnam have been learned and Americans will ensure that the United States maintains a foreign policy that is timely and wise and a military force that is competent, alert, and powerful enough either to deter or quickly win any future wars. The late Marguerite Higgins makes such a plea in her thoughtful book *War in Korea*.

History books dealing with the period leading up to the Korean War tell little of conditions that existed at the time within South Korea itself. We who served in the American occupation forces in South Korea knew nothing of the government policies and military strategies being played out in Washington, DC, and Tokyo, Japan, but we knew a great deal about the small world of South Korea in which we were participants. It was clear to us that South Korea was in turmoil.

Without question, the enlisted men with whom I lived recognized that war was coming. This view was based on personal observations and information from other enlisted men who had served in other parts of South Korea. Most serious to us were stories of the continuing fire fights and armed raids across the 38th parallel that were related by soldiers who had been in the area. We knew these were going on. As time passed, these fights grew in scope and frequency (see both Cumings and Lee).

We also noted our broken down vehicles, shortage of troops, lack of heavy weapons, and most important, the complete lack of defense planning or battle training. These problems were so obvious that we gave up hope in the competence of our American commanders. We felt, rightly or wrongly, that in the event of an invasion from the north, our small group would be abandoned.

We also wondered how much respect our enemies to the north had for the few dirty, poorly equipped American troops that occupied our part of South Korea. We could not believe that we were part of the same army that had only three years earlier won a bitter war against Japan. I can only conclude that we, the soldiers, saw and recognized what was happening. The 63rd Infantry Regiment was no longer the proud and powerful organization that had fought the Japanese in the Philippines. Only a ghost remained.

Relations between the Korean people and the American occupation forces in Korea were not good when I arrived to begin my tour of duty in January 1947. At that time, enlisted personnel had no way of knowing the reasons for the difficulties. Our superior officers seldom talked to us, and when they did, we learned nothing about current affairs or our mission in South Korea. Neither the Army newspaper, *Stars and Stripes*, nor the local army radio station in Chonju, WLKJ, carried any substantive news. Thus, rank and file soldiers had no real concept of the full extent of the terrible shortages of food or the political unrest that beset the people of South Korea.

The result was that soldiers tended to misinterpret the behavior of the Korean people. Stories and experiences involving the pilferage of food, clothing, and fuel by Koreans were seen by soldiers as inherent dishonesty, poor moral character, and disrespect for Americans.

The soldiers I knew felt that our own lack of bare essentials was caused primarily by the Koreans who, as the soldiers said, "stole everything they could get their hands on." Had we known that all of the shortages, both military and civilian, were largely the result of failure on the part of the top United States political planners and military commanders, we might have treated the Korean people with more concern and empathy

Since the end of the Korean War in 1953, South Korea (Republic of Korea) has passed through stages of rigged elections and riots. Nevertheless, with the assistance of the United States, it has grown from a devastated country into a modern democracy. It is populated by hard working, free people with high moral standards.

South Korea is prosperous, with paved roads, modern railroads, clean cities, thriving agriculture, and a growing industrial base. This rise from the ashes of war is a tribute to the Korean people who have survived a brutal 40-year Japanese occupation, a 5-year, bungled American occupation, and the devastating 3-year Korean War.

Unfortunately, Korea remains today a divided country, with the people of South Korea living under continuing threat from the warlike Communist government of North Korea.

HISTORY OF THE
63RD INFANTRY REGIMENT

The following is a copy of a mimeographed pamphlet that was available to soldiers stationed at Camp Hillenmeyer, Korea, in 1947. It is a brief history of the 63rd Infantry Regiment. The only reference indicating its source is a byline at the end of the document indicating that it was prepared and reproduced by the 69th Engineer Topo Company, 24th Corps.

DEDICATED
to
OFFICERS AND MEN
of the
63rd INFANTRY WHO SHED
THEIR BLOOD IN BATTLE

MABUHAY

FORWARD

The complete Regimental Coat of Arms of the 63rd Infantry is shown on the cover. The Shield was approved for the Regiment by the War Department not long after the end of World War I. Recommendations have been made to the War Department for the approval of the Crest and Motto which are based on the fighting record of the 63rd Infantry in World War II.

The Crest, consisting of a Malayan tiger at bay symbolizes the Regiment's bitterest fighting, when troops of the Japanese 14th Area Army under the command of General Tomayuki Yamashita, commonly known as the "Tiger of Malaya," were engaged and defeated throughout Luzon, Philippine Islands. At the time of the cease fire order on 15 August 1945, the 63rd Infantry was actively driving towards General Yamashita's Headquarters in the Mountain Province of Northern Luzon.

The Motto consists of the word "Mabuhay" in blue letters on a silver scroll. The word "Mabuhay" is a Tagalog word meaning "Long Live." It was spontaneously adopted as a victory cry by the men of the Regiment while fighting with the help of Filipino guerrillas during the Luzon Campaign.

REGIMENTAL DAY

On 12 July 1945, troops of the 63rd Infantry Regiment captured KIANGAN, high in the wild and mountainous Ifugao Province in Northern Luzon, P.I. The capture of the town climaxed a sustained 30 days' drive against bitter Japanese Resistance. KIANGAN was the last great enemy stronghold to fall on Luzon, and for months previously had been the Headquarters of General Yamashito, Supreme Japanese Commander in the Philippines. To the men of the 63rd Infantry, the fall of KIANGAN marked the end of the bloody, but victorious campaign; to Yamashita it spelled final and utter defeat.

In order to commemorate the Regiment's brilliant combat record on Luzon, the twelfth day of July was designated as Regimental Day.

BRIEF HISTORY OF THE 63rd INFANTRY REGIMENT
(1 June 1917 to 1 January 1946)

Let us go back to the year 1917. The 63rd Infantry, a World War I unit of the 11th Division, was organized at the Presidio of San Francisco, California, on 1 June, 1917. A cadre from the 12th Infantry formed the nucleus of the new Regiment. It did not see duty overseas during the First World War, and after seeing some service in California and New York, was subsequently demobilized at Plattsburg Barracks, New York, on 31 July 1922. On 6 May 1941, a cadre consisting of the 1st Battalion, 3rd Infantry, arrived at Fort Leonard Wood, Missouri, and became the reactivated 63rd Infantry on 1 June 1941. Two months later, the Regiment participated in the Louisiana maneuvers, returning to Fort Leonard Wood in early October. When World War II was declared, the 63rd Infantry furnished two full Regimental cadres to the expanding Army of the United States.

In September 1942, the Regiment left for two months of maneuvers in Tennessee. In December 1942, a permanent change of station was made to the Desert Training Center, located in the Great Imperial Desert of California. After a few months of desert training, the Regiment underwent an intensive and rigorous training schedule prior to going overseas. On 21 July 1943, the 63rd Infantry left California for the island of Oahu, Territory of Hawaii.

The Regiment stayed 6 months in Hawaii. While there, each man went through a vigorous course in jungle tactics at the Jungle Training School which the Regiment constructed. This school drew a commendation from the War Department.

The Regiment embarked at Honolulu Harbor on 18 January 1944. For the next twelve days the Regiment was alone on the Pacific Ocean aboard the S.S. Monterey. On 30 January, two destroyer escorts joined the ship and conducted her through the Coral Sea to a safe anchorage in Milne Bay, New Guinea. On 8 June, the Regiment moved again, this time into the combat zone at Maffin Bay, Dutch New Guinea — near Wadke Island. It was at this time that the names of Lone Tree Hill, Hill 225, and Hill 265 were engraved in the history of the 63rd. It was here that the Regiment assisted in the defeat of the crack 36th Japanese Infantry Division. As a reward for their exemplary conduct in action against the enemy, the men and officers of the Regiment were awarded the Combat Infantry Badge. On 16 July, the 63rd Infantry was relieved by the 167th Infantry.

After a brief rest, the Regiment embarked for Sansapor, Dutch New Guinea. For one month the doughboys patrolled the beaches and the interior, successfully cutting off elements of the Jap 35th Infantry Division attempting to retreat from Manokwari to Serong. The Regiment then underwent a rigorous training program for the M-1 operation — namely the invasion of Luzon, the largest of the Philippine Islands.

The 63rd Infantry in I Corps reserve landed on White Beach, Lingayen Gulf, on 10 January 1945 and assembled at Alacan. In the initial struggle to enlarge the army beachhead, the Regiment got its first taste of enemy artillery and fought one of the bloodiest actions of the Pacific War. After capturing the key heights southeast of Rosario, the Regimental Commander received the following from Major General Innis (Bull) Swift, Commanding General I Corps: "Please express to each officer and each enlisted man of your command my sincere personal appreciation for the excellent manner in which they have performed a most difficult task. Your precarious advance over open terrain and the scaling of hill masses commanded by enemy forces on the summits, in the face of intense small arm, mortar, and artillery fire, was a magnificent display of courage and determination. The aggressiveness, skill, and gallantry displayed deserve only the highest praise. I know that you are proud of your command, and that each individual in the command is proud of it and determined that in the future the high standards which they have attained in this operation will be exceed, if that is possible."

The 6th Infantry Division commander at this time, Major General Edwin D. Patrick, who was later killed during the Shimbu Line fighting, had this to say: "The aggressive and determined spirit shown by the officers and men of the 63rd are worthy of high praise and testify to the fine spirit [sic] de corps of our troops. I too wish to add my commendation for your gallant action." After the savage battle for Rosario during which the bulk of the Jap 58th IMB and 23rd Infantry Division were wiped out, the Regiment took part in the Munoz-Abar II - San Jose battle which was climaxed by the complete annihilation of a reinforced tank Regiment of the Jap 2nd Armored Division. The Regiment then went on to capture Rizal and drive east to Baler Bay on the eastern coast of Luzon, to complete the isolation of Jap troops in Northern Luzon from those to the south.

After a brief rest, the Regiment moved in February to the vicinity of Novaliches, northeast of Manila, in preparation for the next operation. East of the Regiment lay the Sierra Madre Mountains. Here Japanese General Tomoyuki Yamashita, "Tiger of Malaya", had set up an elaborate defense, later known as the Shimbu Line. From 21 February to the end of April, the Regiment hammered the Shimbu Line, capturing Montalban, Burgos, Kearns Knob, and Hill 400 in the center of the line, and holding them despite constant artillery and heavy mortar fire and fanatical counter-attacks by a desperate foe. The Regiment also captured the key strong-hold of Mount Metaba and the bloody crests of Objectives "A", "B" and "X", and assisted in the capture of the great hill mass, Mount Paoawagan. Another laurel was added to the wreath of the 63rd when the newspapers released their headlines - "63rd Infantry cracks vaunted Shimbu Line."

On 30 April, the Regiment was relieved in this sector and given the mission of mopping up in the hills west of Fort Stetsenburg and Clark Field, on Corregidor Island, and on the Bataan Peninsula. After a breathing spell of comparatively light action, the Regiment was assigned to the mission of taking Kiangan, high in the mountains of Northern Luzon, where General Yamashita, Supreme Commander of the Philippines, was making his last stand.

On 14 June, leading elements of the Regiment left the town of Bagabag in the Cagayan Valley, moving north along Highway

4 and crossing the Lamut River. Determined resistance was encountered during the advance into the mountains. Early in July, the Regiment reached Lanes Ridge, the enemy's main defensive position on the road to Kiangan. This razor-back ridge was taken only after a prolonged and savage hand-to-hand struggle, during which the remainder of the combat effectiveness of the Jap 105th Infantry Division were eliminated.

Here is what the Commanding General of the 6th Infantry Division had to say: "Your Regiment has just completed a difficult task - the seizure of Kiangan which until recently was the headquarters of the Japanese 14th Army commanded by General Yamashita, Supreme Commander of the Japanese troops in the Philippines. The 25 mile drive of the 63rd Infantry from the Lamut River to Kiangan was made in 26 days over torturous mountain terrain against a tenacious, and determined foe who died to the last man. The fortitude, determination and skill displayed by your command during this advance deserves high praise. I therefore wish to commend the officers and men of the 63rd Infantry for their gallant action and to express my appreciation for a job well done." Signed, Charles E. Hurdis, Major General, U.S. Army.

On 15 August 1945, the World War II ended; that day found elements of the 63rd Infantry still up in the front lines. The bloody Luzon campaign was over. The 63rd had earned a fighting reputation and had a made a glorious combat record. The cost of these laurels were not light, however, as the Regiment had almost 1400 battle casualties on Luzon, including 303 dead.

Early in September, the Regiment moved again, this time to San Fernando, La Union, Philippine Islands, where preparations for the move to Korea were started. On 5 October, loading began, and on 10 October, the Regiment sailed from San Fernando Harbor. During the voyage, the Regiment had a few days of rough seas caused by the typhoon that hit Okinawa, 14 October 1945. On 18 October, the Regiment landed at Inchon, Korea, and immediately entrained for the trip to Cholla Pukto Province where the "Fighting 63rd" began its first occupation mission.

The entire province of Cholla Pukto (North) was assigned to the 63rd as its zone of occupation. The 1st Battalion took over the Iri-Chonju-Chinan-Namwon sector; the 2nd Battalion, the Chongup-Kochang-Puan sector; and the 3rd Battalion, the Kunsan-Kumje sector. Initially the Regimental Command Post was established at Kunsan, but was later moved to Chonju, the capital of the province. Anti-tank and Cannon Companies and the Regimental Medical Detachment also were stationed at Kunsan, while Service Company set up their installations at Iri.

First priority mission of the Regiment was to disarm and evacuate to Japan all Japanese army and navy forces in its zone. This important job was done rapidly and efficiently and was completed by November. Thousands of Jap Troops, including the bulk of the 150th and 160th Jap Infantry Divisions were disarmed and evacuated from the Province. At the same time the Regiment took over the job of guarding vast stores of Japanese army supplies and equipment, including everything from airplane engines to horse shoe nails. After inventorying these stores, the 63rd began the difficult task of destroying all warlike materials and converting to civilian use all supplies and equipment suitable for peacetime pursuits.

Another important mission assigned the Regiment was the handling of all displaced persons in its zone. By 10 December 1945, 98% of the 30,000 Japanese civilians residing in the Regimental zone had been evacuated to Japan. The Regiment also fell heir to the task of guarding the large amount of Japanese private and government-owned property in the area, pending its final disposition. Early in December, the port of Kunsan was designated as a main port of entry for Korean repatriates returning from Japan and China, and by 31 December, operations were in full swing, over 35,000 Koreans having been processed through the port up to that date.

Probably the most difficult mission assigned the Regiment in Korea was the establishment of Military Government. For this purpose, specially trained Military Government units were attached to the 63rd Infantry to operate the government of the Province and its 14 Guns (Counties) which totaled 1,674,692 in population. By the end of the year, Military Government with the backing of the 63rd was firmly established in Cholla North Province and the Regiment was well on the way towards the goal of preparing the Korean people for self-government.

UNIT CITATIONS

By Paragraph 5 War Department GO 11, dated 30 January 1946, the 2nd Battalion was awarded the Presidential Unit Citation for outstanding performance of duty in action against the enemy on Lanes Ridge (on road to Kiangan) Luzon, Philippine Islands, 23 June-7 July 1945.

By Paragraph 7 War Department GO 45 dated 15 May 1946, the 3rd Battalion was awarded the Presidential Unit Citation for outstanding performance of duty in action against the enemy northeast of Montalban, Rizal Province, Luzon, Philippine Islands, 23 February-1 March 1945.

The Commanding General, 6th Infantry Division, cited other units of the 63rd Infantry for distinguished performance of duty in the actions listed below, and has recommended to the War Department that these units be awarded a Presidential Unit Citation.

Unit Cited	Action
63rd Infantry Regiment	Lingayen Gulf - Rosario Luzon, P.I., 14-29 January 1945
1st Battalion	Mt. Mataba (Shimbu Line), Luzon, P.I.,l 10-17 April 1945

DECORATIONS

Members of the Regiment earned the following awards during World War II:

Distinguished Service Cross	2
Silver Star	160
Oak Leaf Cluster to Silver Star	4
Bronze Star Medal	762
Oak Leaf Cluster to Bronze Star Medal	42
Soldiers Medal	2
Air Medal	2

IN MEMORIAM

The Regiment suffered the following battle casualties in World War II:

	Dead	Wounded
New Guinea	30	119
Luzon, P.I.	303	1087
	333	1206

May those brave souls buried on New Guinea and Luzon, and at sea, rest forever in peace.

Finis

PREPARED AND REPRODUCED BY 69TH ENGR. TOPO. CO. - XXIV CORPS

ADDITIONAL NOTES

In 1947, the the 63rd Infantry Regiment plus two other regiments, the 1st Infantry and the 20th Infantry, made up the 6th Infantry Division. At that time, the occupation forces in Korea were composed of the 6th and 7th Infantry Divisions. These two Divisions were under the command of the 24th Corps headquartered in Seoul, Korea.

The U.S.Army Center of Military History provided the following information on the activities of both the 63rd Infantry Regiment and the 6th Division from 1945 to the present.

63rd Infantry Regiment

October 18, 1945	Arrived Inch'on, Korea.
October 19, 1945	Arrived Kunsan, Korea.
January 1, 1949	Inactivated.
October 4, 1950	Reactivated at Fort Ord, California, as a training regiment.
April 3, 1956	Inactivated.

6th Division

October 18, 1945	Arrived Korea.
January 10, 1949	Inactivated.
October 4, 1950	Activated Fort Ord, California.
April 3, 1956	Inactivated.
November 24, 1967	Activated Fort Campbell, Kentucky.
July 25, 1968	Inactivated.
March 23, 1986	Activated Fort Richardson, Alaska.
August 16, 1990	Moved to Fort Wainwright, Alaska.

Little more of the history of the 63rd Infantry Regiment or the 6th Division is available. There is a short, but very nicely written, review of the activities of the 63rd Infantry Regiment covering the period 1941 to 1947 by a soldier who served in Company M from July 1941 through November 1945. The complete reference for this 20-page booklet is William L. West, 9213 Wabaday, St. Louis, MO 63114. *The 63rd Infantry Regiment.* Goodale House Printing, 9425 Lackland Road, St. Louis, MO 63114, telephone (314) 426-3449.

Also of interest is the *Sightseer* published by the National Association of the 6th Infantry Division, 5649 South 39th Avenue, Minneapolis, MN 55417. The *Sightseer* is published about four times a year and includes news from and about veterans of the division.

APPENDIX B

References and Recommended Reading

Academy of Korean Studies. 1982. *Reflections on a Century of United States Korean Relations.* New York, NY: University Press of America.

Brzezinski, Zbigniew. 1986. *Game Plan: A Geostrategic Framework for the Conduct of the U.S.- Soviet Contest.* Boston, MA: The Atlantic Monthly Press.

Cumings, Bruce. 1990. *The Origins of the Korean War, Volume II: 1947-1950.* Princeton, NJ: Princeton University Press.

Deutscher, Isaac. 1966. *Stalin: A Political Biography.* 2nd Ed. New York, NY: Oxford University Press.

Ferrell, Robert, Editor. 1980. *Off the Record: The Private Papers of Harry S. Truman.* New York, NY: Harper and Row Publishers.

Higgins, Marguerite. 1951. *War in Korea: The Report of a Woman Combat Correspondent.* Garden City, NY: Doubleday and Company, Inc.

Korean Overseas Information Service. 1995. *Facts about Korea*. Seoul, Korea: Samhwa Printing Company.

Lee Suk Bok. 1987. *The Impact of U.S. Forces in Korea*. Washington, DC: National Defense University Press.

Matloff, Maurice, General Editor. *American Military History*. 1969. Office of the Chief of Military History, United States Army, Washington, DC: U.S. Government Printing Office.

McLogan, Russell E. 1997. *Boy Soldier — Coming of Age During World War II*. In press.

Munschauer, John L. 1996. *World War II Cavalcade: An Offer I Couldn't Refuse*. Manhattan, KS: Sunflower University Press

Nilsen, Robert. 1988. *South Korea Handbook*. Chico, CA: Moon Publs.

Sawyer, Major Robert K. 1988. *Military Advisors in Korea: KMAG in Peace and War*. Washington, DC: Center of Military History, United States Army.

Smith, Robert. 1982. *MacArthur in Korea: The Naked Emperor*. New York, NY: Simon and Schuster.

Stone, I. F. 1952. *The Hidden History of the Korean War*. Boston, MA: Little Brown and Company.

West, William L., 9213 Wabaday, St. Louis, MO 63114. *The 63rd Infantry Regiment*. St.Louis, MO: Goodale House Printing.

White, Theodore H., ed. 1972. *The Stilwell Papers: General Joseph W. Stilwell's Iconoclastic Account of America's Adventures in China*. New York, NY: Schocken Books.

INDEX OF PEOPLE